# 1,800 Miles

# 1,800 Miles

Striving to End Sexual Violence, One Step at a Time

JOSHUA DANIEL PHILLIPS

New York

# 1,800 Miles
## Striving to End Sexual Violence, One Step at a Time

ISBN 978-1-60037-677-1

Library of Congress Control Number: 2009931649

# MORGAN · JAMES
**THE ENTREPRENEURIAL PUBLISHER**

Morgan James Publishing, LLC
1225 Franklin Ave., STE 325
Garden City, NY 11530-1693
Toll Free 800-485-4943
www.MorganJamesPublishing.com

In an effort to support local communities, raise awareness and funds, Morgan James Publishing donates one percent of all book sales for the life of each book to Habitat for Humanity. Get involved today, visit **www.HelpHabitatForHumanity.org.**

For Rachel

who always reminds me that it's not about me

*What legacy is to be found in silence?*

*bell hooks*

# Table of Contents

# Introduction

One of my goals in life is to find myself written into the pages of *Time* magazine. This goal is desired not so much for societal approval, but rather for the novelty of it all. Furthermore, I don't really care when it happens, just so long as it happens. For that, I suppose I really don't care if *I* find myself in the pages insomuch that I am in the pages. Essentially, they can cover my story once I'm dead or at least put a few short lines about me on the *Milestone* page, which is really just a fancy celebrity word for obituary. If I'm really lucky, I've always liked the idea of being one of the *100 Most Influential People of the Year*, but I'm not sure my influence will reach those types of epic standards for credentials.

Either way, there's a certain type of enthusiasm that rises up within me when I know I've done something worthy of making the news. Whether the news covers it or not is inconsequential. The last time I made the press was just a few months ago when I got tickets to go the inauguration of President Barack Obama. Although I really didn't do anything newsworthy to obtain the tickets, like becoming the first black United States President for instance, it was nice to know that someone wanted to talk to me about my experiences.

This whole concept of "my experiences" is where this story begins. Or rather *how* this story begins. Last summer I, along with two friends, embarked on an eighteen-hundred-mile journey from Miami to Boston to raise awareness about sexual violence – on foot. Later we will get in to the particulars of how such a journey like this begins, but for now it is only important that you to know that it happened.

Anyway, the three of us walked the East Coast of the United States of America and *Time* magazine didn't care. In fact, no national media outlets cared and only a very few, perhaps a dozen or so, local media outlets stretching along the entire East Coast cared. Therefore, my reasons for writing this book are twofold. First, it is important to me that some of my own stories and experiences are recorded in the pages of history. You know, just in case I accidentally have children one day and they want to know what sort of cool things their dad did before he became old and boring. This reason could also be translated as my selfish desire of wanting the approval of my hypothetical kids and for them to know that in my youth I was cool, not old and not boring. It must be rather rewarding to a father when his child recognizes that at some point in time their dear old dad willingly took risks and embodied nonconformity as a way of rebellion against conventional wisdom. Either way, both motives produce the same outcome – writing some stories for those who come after me on the family tree.

Second, I think our message for the walk was and still is extremely important. Truth be told, writing is hard and I would rather tell my stories, as opposed to typing them. This is why I put so much effort into obtaining speaking engagements around the country rather than investing effort in getting multiple book contracts. But as many of my close friends remind me, "It's not about you!" As deflating as this can sound to my ego on some days, what they mean is that finishing this book isn't about me achieving the goal of becoming a published author. If I fail at completing this book, then I cause failure to more than just myself and my unstroked ego. Because of the blessed position I have been placed in, I have a responsibility to write this book because of what has been shared with me. If I learned anything on that trip up the East Coast, it was this: *my ambitions to walk were far less important than the message I carried.* In fact, in relation to the accomplishments of other people we met along the way, walking eighteen-hundred-miles isn't even really all that impressive, let alone valuable. Instead, the stories I heard and the experiences I had on the trip with those I encountered are what remain valuable, and they are the stories that deserve to be told. They are the stories that deserve to be listened to. Therefore, writing this book is for those who shared their stories with me while I walked the East Coast and for anyone who has ever been subjected to acts of sexual violence.

I admit that there are moments when I wish I was a powerful writer for all the selfish reasons: money, power, fame, and admiring women fans (women are really more of a hope rather than a reality for most heterosexual male writers, I think). If not for these reasons, then I suppose that I sometimes simply want to be considered poetic and articulate with words. However, in this moment, I just want to become a writer who can write something captivating in hopes of bringing attention, understanding, and compassion to all those affected by sexual violence. I hope that writing this book will act as a catalyst that aids in continuing the conversations we had while on the trip – conversations that I hope will reach far beyond the edges of this book's cover and into our communities. Conversations produced all in the effort of ending sexual violence – one step at a time.

# Walk

I n and of itself, walking is an rather undramatic event. Seriously, how often do we watch the Super Bowl of walking? Some would even classify walking as boring, dull, and uneventful – kind of like golf. In fact, watching someone walk is exactly like watching someone golf, given that you turn away right before every tee shot. I don't say this to maliciously bash the sport of golf, but just to point out how little excitement there is between each shot. If I were to make a conservative guess, I would say that golf is about 98 percent walking.

Most of us who are blessed enough to have legs probably engage in the act of walking every day – even if it is only to go from our bedroom to the bathroom on a lazy Saturday afternoon. But I propose that walking can be so much more than just a convenience, especially if it is accompanied by large camping backpacks and a group of people with matching bright teal shirts. This idea of bright teal shirts is where the thought of walking to raise awareness about sexual violence entered my life. Well, maybe not the bright teal shirts per se, but at least the idea of attention calling acts; acts that are so colorfully decorated and unusual that the public would not be able to ignore them or the message they carried.

Our message was simple. We wanted people who had been hurt by sexual violence to know that someone cared. Furthermore, we wanted to educate those not directly affected by sexual violence about how the act of sexual violence has a deep and ugly history that undermines the everyday of our existence and is still pervasive throughout our communities. And here, for our purposes, I feel it is important to note that we deliberately chose the phrase "sexual violence" to be all-inclusive of any act where sexual dominance is the goal to be achieved through power and control. For the three of us, this term included, but was not limited to, sexual assault, domestic violence, and child molestation. Without getting into the details and histories of these acts themselves (there are plenty of other books for that) all one needs to recognize is that sexual violence happens every day. Sexual violence happens to all different types of people from all different walks of life. In fact, sexual violence may be the single most indiscriminate act in U.S. American culture, as it successfully transcends race, ethnicity, gender, socio-economics, geographic location, and sexual orientation, silently assaulting the souls, spirits, and existence of millions of everyday folks around us on a daily basis.

Knowing that sexual violence still exists in our communities, I have and still continue to wrestle with the question of how to address the issue. Being perceived as and socially categorized as a "women's issue," how does a man aid in the fight against sexual violence? Well, I would recommend that the first thing every man needs to do is pay his respects to the women who have been on the front lines of these violent battlefields for generations, yet went unnoticed because our culture found sexual violence too taboo a subject to discuss openly in schools, churches, media, and politics. Even more, I would go so far as to say that because of the patriarchal domination of our culture, any issues that more greatly affect women are often pushed out of the center and marginalized at the sides only to be replaced by "more important," man-centered issues. This then leads to my conclusion that, yes, if sexual violence happened more frequently to men like me who can identify with echelons of privilege, the issue would receive far greater attention, more radical social demonstration, and political legislation would be put in place in order to "stop the violence" and "take back the night." Yet this is not the case, and instead women are forced into isolated suffering with little help from the systemic patriarchal power structures that hold the key to societal resources that could more quickly put an end to this grave injustice that repeatedly assaults the womb of our human existence.

What continues to be even more problematic about the act of sexual violence in a male dominated culture is that victims of the crime are rendered silent by patriarchal norms. During sexual advances, women are taught to be submissive and passive when it comes to defining their sexual boundaries. Therefore, a woman may literally be scared speechless and unable to raise objections as her body freezes in an attempt to survive the attack. I use the phrase "survive the attack" to bring attention to the overwhelming physical strength the average man has over the average woman. In a consensual setting, the larger sized man may not intimidate the smaller sized woman because communication is happening and the man is not looking to use his size as a sexual advantage. But if the sex is not consensual, it takes very little stretch of the imagination to empathize with one's inability to say "no" if the person out weighs them by 50 – 70 pounds of muscle. Take for example my partner and me. She is an athletically built 5'7" and weighs 130 pounds while I am an athletically built 5'8" and weigh 175 pounds. As strong as she is, if I chose to rape her, she would not be able to physically overpower me. Now imagine the physical intimidation you might feel next to a man who weighs 185, 195, or 205 pounds. For a man my size, this average weight difference would be the equivalent of fighting Mike Tyson. Add in the inebriating effects of alcohol or drugs that aid in facilitating many sexual assaults and people may become virtually defenseless. To add to the subjugation of women, after an act of sexual violence, women are so verbally attacked in the media and in their communities as "attention seeking whores" that they are forced into quiet isolation. With these tactics of victim blaming, it comes as little surprise that the report rates for sexual assault are amazingly low.

In relation to the treatment of perpetrators, what is strikingly convenient for a male in a male-centered culture is when and how the patriarchal system expects a woman to speak up. Patriarchal culture has taught women to shut up and not speak in the classrooms, in the household, and generally in most societal circumstances except when it is convenient for men to assert that a woman should have say "no" during a sexual assault. This creates quite the paradox. As men, we have stolen the voices of women, yet accuse of them of not speaking up. Instead, men need to be held accountable and responsible in creating spaces where women can find their voices so that all women feel comfortable verbally expressing their consent or refusal during sex. It would do us well to remember that consensual sex between any partners of any gender should emotionally, physically, and legally require the presence of a "yes," not simply the absence of a "no."

Next, we should recognize that women have been, and most likely always will be, the first respondents to any sexually violent act where the survivor wishes to seek out help. This is not to say that men are incapable of responding to the needs of a survivor, but to simply realize that it makes sense that a survivor, who is most likely female, would want to talk to another female since the probability of the perpetrator being male is approaching absolute. Therefore, because I am a man and

I am less likely to deal directly with survivors of sexual violence, my time may be better spent in two other areas. First, my primary objective is in supporting my female colleagues. In essence, men need to learn how to take orders from women and do whatever is asked of them to best support their female advocates. This is not because sexual violence is solely a "women's issue," but because women endure patriarchal oppression daily and therefore are best positioned to understand how to work against our rape culture. Men need to recognize the possibility that they may not know what is best for a woman after a sexually violent act has taken place and therefore, we should more actively engage in the practice of humble servitude. My second objective is education – both for myself and the public.

When I first began to educate myself on the issue of sexual violence, one thing I was constantly confronted with was the fact that all cultural, political, and social systems are weaved into the fabric of our everyday lives. Contemporary culture floods our lives with half-naked (and fully-naked) women, objectification, dehumanization, pornography, sexism, submission, and violence. Analyzed as a sum of all these parts, it is reasonable – although unpopular – to say that the act of rape is supported by our culture. If unchallenged, these systems remain intact and continue forward undetected while simultaneously swallowing up any protest that may call for serious cultural rehab. Essentially, the rapes keep happening and collectively we ignorantly question "why?" When contemplating the issue of sexual violence, the question I continuously pose to myself is, "How can I push these cultural boundaries of silence in a way to draw attention to the issue of sexual violence?" The answer I came to was that in order to produce real change (or at least produce conversations about real change) the systems in which I operate everyday should be constantly questioned and social boundaries should be pushed. In essence, as a male with access to systemic power and privilege I need to call attention to cultural systems and critically deconstruct any parts that may be considered sexist, racist, violent, homophobic, et cetera.

Without a doubt, pushing these boundaries can be, and in all probability will be, dangerous because it requires a person to present unpopular information to people who may be complacent with their current situations. For one, no one wants to be bothered with ideas about cultural change if the status quo of that culture provides them an enjoyable and fulfilling lifestyle. Who wants to hear conversations about sweat shops if their name brand sneakers are making them look cool on the basketball court? Second, men who are not survivors of sexual violence and who do not engage in the act of sexual violence oftentimes do not want to be hassled with a perceived "women's issue." Now, I do not blame men *entirely* for their apathy, but I do not excuse them for it either. Seeing that no one is above their own socialization, it seems reasonable that men would want to stay within the confines of their categorized box and chose not to get involved with the issue of sexual violence because that it what culture teaches them to do. Men hold onto the mentality that because they are not committing these acts of violence against women, they have somehow done their part in stopping violence against women. And while I commend them for respecting the sexual choices of women, I also want to offer them an alternative position as opposed to their current position of complacent silence. I want to ask them to join other men in helping to stop the act of sexual violence. Just because I as a man don't rape women doesn't mean that the women I care about in my life are immune to the criminal choices of bad men. For this reason alone, men should be concerned. While fear of social rejection is a real emotion when it comes to pushing boundaries, we cannot allow fear to push us into indifference. Reminded by numerous activists both past and present, indifference to evil is more evil than evil itself and being silent will not put end to the violent acts that threaten our mothers, our sisters, our partners, and our friends everyday.

Too many folks are opting to fit in and remain silent instead of speaking up and risking social rejection and consequentially convince others that silence is the popular choice. Therefore, the movement to end sexual violence needs to create a catalyst that will entice others to join the fight. Part of what is needed is new and creative ways to approach the issue and shift our thinking in order to successfully operate across various demographics. I understand here that my efforts cannot simply be a plea in hopes that those who hurt and abuse women will stop. First, I seriously doubt that those who chose to hurt women are interested in reading this book and second, I doubt that reading this book will change their polluted minds. Instead, my efforts are better spent at recruiting. I wish to recruit good people who are indifferent to the issue of sexual violence to courageously stand up and speak out against sexual violence.

Speaking out against the culturally accepted norms pushes boundaries and people who push boundaries are courageous. Everyday, people courageously struggle against oppressive systems desperately desiring to enact change. Most often these folks represent demographic groups that have been pushed, shoved, and forced to the margins of society; at the intersections of their identities include women of color, white women, people with disabilities, members of the gay, lesbian, bisexual, and transgender community, those who are non-English speaking, and those who live in poverty. They are the truth tellers who force us to examine our own conformity and they live as an example of proactive change as opposed to reactive damage control. Their confrontation may be taxing, but their confrontation is the only way to spark change and dismantle systems of violence that hurt those we care about. For us, this walk was our attempt at being proactive and a way to voice our opposition to hurt, abuse, and pain. But it was more than just a protest; it had to be more than a protest because protests offer no solutions to the problem. This walk was proactive recruitment. Our solution was to recruit others to speak up in the face of sexual violence. In a system so strategically laced with conformity and complacency, we attempted to break the mold of social norms through the radical act of walking.

Well, maybe walking isn't so radical, but that's not the point.

The point is that the act of walking called attention to ourselves and subsequently called attention to the issue of sexual violence. In a culture virtually absent of cross-country walkers who willingly walk your highways and through your neighborhoods – whether they be rural communities or city streets – we knew or at least naively hoped that walkers who stopped by your homes, restaurants, country-clubs, and churches would be noticed. We knew that we would not fit in and not fitting in was the most important part of this social experiment. By not fitting in we would draw attention to ourselves, spark curiosity, and get people to ask questions. And it was in the peeked interest of our audience that we would be able to take the focus off of ourselves and have meaningful conversations about the issue of sexual violence.

The following is a collection of some of those stories as told from only one walker's perspective – the perspective of a struggling man trying to do what he can with what he has where he's at. In the interest of not speaking for the two women on the trip – which would only cause a paradoxical conversation about the sexism laced throughout a book that aims to address just that particular issue – I will only assert these experiences as my own knowing full well that Kate and Rebecca would do a much better job narrating their own journey.

**Note: Some of the names and locations throughout the following stories have been changed to respect people's confidentiality. Other than a few name changes here and there, the following is an accurate account of my experiences in the style of creative non-fiction. So please don't come after me for falsification – especially you Oprah because you have the power to ruin someone's entire career.

# Where Do We Even Begin?

People always ask whose inebriated idea it was to walk from Miami to Boston. To be honest, walking countless miles across the country for an elongated length of time wasn't our idea at all. It wasn't even an original idea that had been dreamed up during late night conversations at the bar where everything from quitting school and moving to West Texas to become a cattle rancher to renouncing all of one's possessions to go live in a Buddhist monastery seem like reasonable and, at times, ingenious ideas. No, walking across the country to raise awareness about sexual violence had already been done.

About seven years, before the three of us stole the idea and claimed ownership, four guys from our college had walked from San Francisco to Washington D.C. to raise awareness about violence against women. During our time as undergraduates, one or two of them would occasionally return to the advocacy group we belonged to and tell us campfire stories about their heroic tales of marching through the desolate landscapes of Nevada, Colorado, Nebraska, and Iowa all in the name of ending sexual violence. While I still cling to some of their overly romanticized myths and legends, I do occasionally wonder what sort of folks and livestock they were preaching to in Western Nebraska. Either way, I truly appreciate the courageous path they set before us.

Naturally, significant parts of their journey were told and retold and of course some of these parts became elaborated, exaggerated, and probably even fabricated as all stories tend to do after the telling and retelling of them over a period of several years. But to get caught up in the details of fact finding only makes the critic less satisfied. I say, let the details fall where they may and allow me to benefit from the spirit of the tale. After all, who am I to judge someone else's experience? If that's how they remembered it – fully inclusive of ten-foot-tale mountain men and hairy little helper elves – then so be it. It's not my job to point out fallacies. Instead it's my job to be entertained and inspired.

Inspired I was. From the moment I first heard their stories as a sophomore in college, I yearned for the opportunity to tell my own audacious stories and to create my own gallant memories. And so I tried. Year after year I tried, but to avail. Creating journeys such as this in college proved to be a harder task than expected for a plethora of reasons. A major one being organization…or lack thereof.

I remember the first time a few of us tried to replicate the epic walk. It was in 2004 at the beginning of my junior year. Sitting against the backdrop of a fireplace at a local coffee shop in late October, a few of us sketched out our tentative plans amidst the pungent coffee smell – smells that can only be found in the most pretensions flavors marketed to college towns in an effort to show mom and dad how cultured and well traveled their 18 – 24 year olds can be.

In despite of our lofty goals, the group of us assembled there were at the very least mature enough to realize that if a walk of this size was going to be repeated, then we needed impeccable organization. So with our legal pads in hand, we tirelessly created lists and divided the tasks between the five of us for the next three hours.

In a way, the lists we created were almost comical. Here we were, five college kids with reckless ambitions creating organized lists. The very idea of reckless organization almost seems counterintuitive; an oxymoron of sorts. This wasn't how youthful politico was supposed to happen! Jack Kerouac never created lists before heading out! He just went! At least that's how I like to picture him – the strong-minded bohemian with no list. And this is how I wanted the walk to happen. But then again, we were new at this reckless adventurer thing so maybe we needed a list to coach us into it. Take a small sip now, the hard stuff will come later.

In our defense, and mostly as an excuse, all of this organization as opposed to radicalism was done because it was difficult to break out of our identity. We were college kids trying to stay organized so we could stay on top of our school work and now all of a sudden we were trying to be radical in the name of social change. Perhaps what we needed to do was make an additional list that helped us figure out a way to slowly stop using all lists in a way that never let us know that we were hooked on lists in the first place. Kind of like how nicotine gum helps people stop smoking. At the bottom of our list we could simply write, "Congratulations, you have successfully moved away from using a list."

List or no list, 2004 never happened. Neither did 2005. If something was being planned in 2006, then it fell apart without me because I was out of school and living in Jersey – I hope to write about *that* experience in another book. What remains increasingly disappointing for me is that the reason for the failures was simple: *walking to raise awareness about sexual violence wasn't a priority for any of us.* Sure we grasped onto the spectacle of forever being immortalized as the ones who courageously walked for such a noble cause, but the truth is that we were all too comfortable in our current situations and more realistic options were being paraded before us. At certain times, certain folks got accepted to graduate school and there were other times when folks got job offers. Then there were those of us who were still finishing our undergraduate degrees and when push came to shove we chose not to disrupt the quiet movement of everyday life – that silent timeline that pushes on towards death. It is my suspicion that it is this timeline's stealth quality that forces you to wake-up one day and question, "Why didn't I do that?" But is it really hard to understand how opportune moments for practical resistance slip by? After all, the timeline's silence is what tricks us into thinking we have more time to do all of those reasonable and ingenious ideas that make most of out parents smile and nod on the outside while screaming, "noooooooooo!" in a cave-like fashion on the inside. Well, our parents shouldn't worry too much because most of us don't do any of that crazy stuff anyhow. We're just too busy with the mundane pattern.

When I returned to college in 2007 for graduate school, new faces had been cast across the landscape of my former campus. Fresh faces reminded me of a time when my ideologies were better than my elders and how I was going to live my life differently. A cultural rebel I was and would be. Perhaps this is why I became so enthused about the proposed prospect of once again tediously weeding through the details of tracking across the country. Life was giving me one more chance to pull this feat off before I left college for good.

I remember the first day of planning vividly. Sitting in the library always has this certain effect on me. Libraries heighten my perceptions and just plain make me feel more intelligent – even if my intelligence is not really a factor. Either way, I felt productive that first day of planning. Wadding in what felt like a swimming pool of maps, a male colleague and I attempted to solve geographical math and tried to be reasonable with our objective. Being that this trip had been unsuccessfully planned and canceled several times before, we were intensely concerned about calculating practicality so that it would be impossible to fail again.

What we discovered that day in the library was so simple that it pained me to think about how much time was once wasted on previous planning that only got catalogued in the back of my mind as great ideas that I never made time for. You know, those ideas that one day would be buried six feet underground alongside the thousands, if not millions, of other great ideas that never manifest due to a lack of time, perseverance, or motivation. Yet, I suppose cemeteries are paradoxical like that. They hold so many ideas that people finally have the time to do, but they are now buried under the unsympathetic soil of eternity.

Anyway, I digress. Our conclusion for the walk was this: plan the trip based on time rather than on space. Previous to 2007 we were so hung up on replicating destinations of colossal proportions that we never took a moment to think about an alternative time frame. Now, instead of worrying about getting caught up in someone else's glory of a six month journey from the Pacific to the Atlantic, we were really making this trip our own. Due to the high probability of people dropping-out if in fact the trip interfered with their school schedules, we made the executive decision to walk what we could during summer break. I realize now that this is a rather obvious and most unimpressive answer to an easy question, but then again, references to hindsight are catchy for a reason.

Taking this walk during summer break gave us approximately 100 days to work with. Using what we knew from the previous group's experience, walking 20 miles a day was a reasonable figure. Therefore, basic math illustrated that 100 days x 20 miles a day = 2,000 miles. In the time allotted, we could travel 2,000 miles and make it back in time for the first day of classes. After plowing through atlases and maps, it wasn't long until we decided that the East Coast would be our ideal location. In short, the East Coast is extremely populated and our ultimate goal was to spread awareness about sexual violence to as many people as possible. Although, our journey may not be as impressive mileage wise, we sure as hell wouldn't be bored walking for days and weeks at a time without seeing another human being. Sometimes when I think about the guys who walked from San Francisco to Washington D.C., I like to imagine them having conversations about whose stupid idea it was to walk through the oftentimes desolate landscapes of Nevada, Colorado, Nebraska, and Iowa.

Two-thousand-miles is roughly the distance from Augusta, Maine to Miami, Florida given the turns and contours of the roadways. Originally, we had decided to start in Augusta because we were hoping to end on the doorstep of Miami Ink and get tattoos. We also had high hopes of landing on their television series. I mean, if I worked at Miami Ink, tattooing some college kids who just walked in from Augusta, Maine to raise awareness about sexual violence would be the kind of publicity I would want. However, after a much needed reality check about the weather from an insightful professor of mine, we quickly changed our direction. Instead of walking North to South, it would be more intelligent to walk South to North. Honestly, who wants to walk through South Florida in August? But I'm still up for that tattoo if Miami Ink wants to give me a call.

At this point in time, we had never been so close to making our dream a reality. Now that we had a tentative map and a rough outline of where we needed to be on certain days, buzz began to gather and people took interest. Unfortunately, for the first few weeks in early fall, all that really happened was buzz. Every now and again people would talk to me about their interest, but there was never any committed follow through. Then I met Kate. Kate was one of those fresh faces on campus I had mentioned earlier. She and I only knew about each other through other people, but when she approached me about the trip I knew we both shared the same passion and excitement.

"Hi. I'm Kate. I don't want to impose and I'm not sure if this trip is exclusive, but I heard that you and some other people are planning to do another walk and I wanted to know if I could join."

From that moment forward, Kate's initiative took over and she was in charge, which was fine by me for the simple reason that she enjoyed being organized and I still had bohemian ambitions to the likes of Jack Kerouac. Dusting off the old legal pads, she and I would begin meeting regularly, compose action plans, and think up creative ways to get people's support behind us even if they couldn't walk with us. As a word of advice, if you're ever going to do something big, it's always a good idea to tell a whole bunch of people about it. This way you're more accountable to follow through because quitting is too great an embarrassment. Harsh I know, but it works.

Within a month of planning, there were only three of us walkers left. Even my original partner who helped me map the route had dropped out. I think what proved to be the most vital element for the three of us in terms of being successful was the weekly meetings and accountability. Lists are nice, but without constant check-ins, those lists never get completed. Furthermore, the three of us had gotten extremely close in only a month and gained a heightened sense of obligation to one another and to the cause. It also helped that the three of us were individually stubborn enough to prove everyone wrong who said it couldn't be done. Kate and Rebecca had the extra baggage of proving all the men wrong who said women wouldn't physically last.

By the time Christmas break was upon us we had almost everything in order. We had begun writing support letters to family, friends, businesses, and administration for financial contributions. Research indicated that we would need about $8,000 to make this work. We also pleaded with local sporting goods stores hoping to get some equipment donations. Equipment was expensive and any donations would greatly reduce our overall cost. What may have been the most essential donation we got came from the President's Office at our school. It wasn't that this particular donation was more important or financially greater than the rest, but rather the fact that the donation was specific: *the President's Office was going to buy our plane tickets.*

Up until then the trip never seemed real to me. Sure the trip was obtainable, but it was never tangible. It was as if I could see it, but I could never touch it. I felt this way because, if we needed to, all of those small financial donations could be given back, equipment returned, and orders canceled. In the return of these items, all that would be sacrificed was a portion of my ego during an embarrassing exchange and some awkward conversations. But the commitment of plane tickets seemed so…so permanent. With the purchasing of plane tickets on the horizon, we were now on the cusp of complete submersion and I felt obligated to reach out to any other potential walkers one last time.

Some may not understand my overly zealous recruitment strategies for additional walkers, but for me, I felt that it was my responsibility to make one last announcement about our trip in order to invite all those fair-weather folks who had talked so much about the walk, but had so far failed to commit. I just didn't want anyone to feel left out. Call my sympathy what you will, but I just see it as shameful when people hoard social issues and claim them as their own – unwilling to allow others into the conversation; unwilling to allow others to make a decision about their own circumstances. It's as if some justice seekers feel a sense of entitlement or ownership over something that cannot be owned.

As a man who has never been sexually assaulted and has never felt the oppression that comes with living as a woman in a patriarchal society, I couldn't allow myself to make the ignorant mistake of speaking up for people without first asking for their input. I couldn't have taken this trip with a peace of mind knowing that someone back home wanted to be there with us, but my arrogance and self-righteousness prevented them from joining. How can a man speak up about violence against women and at the same time drown out the voices of all the women around him? Besides, it's not as if I owned the East Coast or the roads I would travel. So on the final days leading up to Christmas break, we made the following announcement to the large group of peer advocates on our campus:

"One week after we return from Christmas break we are buying plane tickets to Miami. Please use the break to talk to family and friends about your decision. Let us know your answer when you return. We don't want to rush people into any decision, but donations are coming in and we need to know how many people to plan for. Everyone is invited and please contact us if you have any questions."

When we returned from Christmas break the numbers remained the same. We bought three tickets out of Detroit and into Miami for May 5, 2008. Due to the lack of airports and scheduling conflicts in Augusta we would be returning to Detroit from Boston on August 5, 2008. Boston is about 200 miles short of Augusta, but it was the last major city that offered reasonable return transportation. Plus, now if you do the math, the title of this book makes a whole lot more sense.

# The First Ten Days

The first ten days were quite possibly some of the most physically grueling days of my life. In short, I hated them. I hated every step that I took and I hated myself for agreeing to such a seemingly tortuous form of transportation and social action; mainly my feet. Seriously, who did I think I was? Well, I suppose I only had myself to blame. Nay saying critics did warn me about the impossibility of our ambitions.

A constant concern often brought to our attention while planning the walk was one of physical capability. One person even thought it necessary to ask us if we knew we needed walking shoes as if we were planning to do the whole thing barefoot or in flip-flops. With my athletic background, I had no problem shrugging off all those who wished to erect stumbling blocks and pessimistic attitudes in front of my chances at large-scale social resistance. In fact, at times I found it humorous the amount of folks who offered advice about how to go about taking on such a daunting task. It was as if overnight several family members, friends, acquaintances, professors, and even complete strangers were suddenly experts at training for a three month walk. To my knowledge, there were only four people within my social network who had any idea what it was like to walk for that amount of distance for that amount of time and none of them were constantly offering up advice about how to go about it. Having now done a walk of this magnitude, there is only one piece of useful advice I have for anyone who wants to repeat the walk or various variations of it: *the first ten days are going to be horrible and there's nothing you can do about it.* By all means, please plan for bigger and better milestones than what we achieved, but do so knowing that there is absolutely nothing in the world that will prepare you for walking 20 miles a day, every day for three consecutive months in a row except for the very act itself. And if you can avoid it, don't listen to people who tell you differently or offer up training advice. Quite frankly, no one has any idea what it's like until they do it.

Every day my feet hurt. And I mean they hurt every day beyond just the first ten days. However, the first ten days were the worst and the pain was indescribable. For the first week and half, it was more than just sore soles at the end of long workouts. It was a constant, shooting pain up through the ankle that incased each foot inside a ball of sharp needles. With every step the needles would drive further and further into my feet until they would poke out the other side. The only thing I could do was walk at an extremely fast pace praying for the end of the day to come quickly. On more than one occasion, this quick pace got me in trouble with my walking partners. I would get so far ahead of them that it was impossible for them to reach me via their yelling and they found this bothersome. Well actually my racing ahead to try and run from the pain in my feet more than bothered them, but I will let your imagination fill in the details of their reactions since they were understandably pissed. Although, their reactions did soon became subdued and after a couple of weeks en route we abandoned the walking side-by-side mentality that made for scenic pictures of team work and perseverance and instead went at our own individual paces. Quite truthfully, once we ran out of things to say and occasionally grew sick of each other, the miles literally grew between us and we decided to just keep our cell phones on in case of a bathroom, or any other, emergency.

Besides the constant physical hurt that Florida's pavement lashed into my feet, Florida's size also hurt my feelings. Florida's size was like a big f-you to start out our journey. Starting up North may have caused heat trouble come late-July, but at least Connecticut looks manageable on a map. Connecticut would have been a good state to slowly coax us into the journey. After four days of traveling up Highway 1, we found ourselves sitting down in a fast-food joint going over the particulars of the map only to discover that we had traveled perhaps three and half inches with about four more feet to go. The impossibility of ever completing this asinine walk began to sink in. It was here, inside the greasy walls of a burger chain, that we decided that should we get *waaaayyyyy* behind schedule we would hitch a ride to Boston in the last week of the trip. Fortunately, those types of rash decisions were months away and in all honesty these "we might not make it" conversations were mostly outlets for blowing off the steam of mental stress brought on by the cruel and defeating appearance of three and half inches.

For those who have never been, walking the coast of Florida is like traveling up one long strip-mall complete with sidewalks, neon-signs, and a beach. It was actually better walking conditions than we could have hoped for. Being that summer break had just begun the place was packed with tourist and local beach-bums. With our giant packs and matching teal shirts, people noticed and flocked to us like junior high kids to a movie theatre showcasing the latest addition in the *High School Musical* saga. You know, just weird enough to cause a little hype. It seemed as if every ten feet or so someone would stop us and ask about what we were doing. At first I was happy about the prospect of illuminating minds and spreading the message of ending sexual violence, but illuminating minds meant sounding like a tape-recorder constantly stuck on repeat while we explained to each new person what we were doing. Soon happiness turned into sheer exhaustion.

The mental game that the map of Florida played with my mind became even more difficult to win when most of the population of South Florida informed us that we wouldn't make it. There is a laidback attitude in South Florida and most people were fairly aloof about our journey and simply brushed us off as naïve kids who wouldn't get any farther than the Florida/Georgia border, if we even made it that far. I wanted to scream in each one of their doubting faces, "Seriously people? That's all the respect and encouragement we get? We've been on the road less than a week and you're not even giving us a chance! I know people who have more faith in the Cubs winning a World Series! At least we have a realistic goal!" In addition to the size of the state and most Floridian's negative attitudes, we were now living the reality that so many speaking stops made for *very* long days.

As is, walking 20 miles a day can take nine to ten hours when you calculate in breaks for rest, food, and the toilet. And nine to ten hours a day is what we planned for. However, talking to as many folks as we did, we were usually on the road for more like thirteen to fourteen hours a day. Though being on my feet all this time wasn't what was all that upsetting; my feet were going to hurt regardless of whether or not I was sitting or standing. But I never accounted for the constant pull of my pack down my entire backside and as cocky as I can be, I ignored the advice of the weird sporting goods' guy at the local camping store who said that one-ounce would feel like one-pound once we had been walking that much. He was right, I was wrong, and it's true. By the end of a long day, my 30-pound pack turned into me giving a piggy back ride to Andre the Giant. So in the future, it's important to remember that regardless of what your gut feeling may tell you about sounding out retail advice, I recommend that everyone sticks around and listens to the weird guys in the store who are trying to sell you retail. All their social awkwardness probably just steams from the fact that they're doing so much product research that they have no time to develop friendly communication skills.

When we originally packed our gear we thought we were fairly frugal in our possessions. Before water, the average pack was less than 25 pounds. Yet, it was surprising when I learned how little I could go with for a whole summer when I had to carry those possessions on my back thirteen hours a day. By the fifth day we had had enough and did some careful inventory of what we had and had not yet used. Some folks might say that day five is too early to tell, but by this time, five days had felt like five weeks and I wasn't about to hold onto that extra book, extra t-shirt, and extra pen on the off chance that I may need it come the Carolinas. I am even willing to gamble that we are living in a time of pen abundance and if we were to stop producing them now, the supply would not dry up for a good 50 years. Using similar logic, I was certain that someone would loan me a pen should the occasion arise for me to write a postcard.

On the sixth morning, four and half inches north of the Miami airport, we stopped by a local UPS. With our needless possessions in tow, we dumped all those unnecessaries into a large brown box and shipped them back to Kate's house. We figured that if we really needed them in the future we could have her folks mail them to a local post-office a few days ahead of us and we'd be able to pick them up. Aside from the aforementioned items, I also sent home my extra pair of shoes. This was probably my most difficult piece of gear to part with (I mean we were walking after all and shoes should be my number one priority), but the weight of hiking shoes is astronomic when you're carrying them on your back 20 miles a day. After sampling both pairs of shoes for the first few days, I became partial to the high-boots over the low shoes. The added support at the ankle made my walking far more enjoyable – and by enjoyable I mean that the pain was less intense up the shins and around the lower calf.

Filling up that ten pound box made us all lighter on our feet. We were now ready to sprint up the East Coast. Unfortunately, the physical impact of the trip wasn't the only obstacle we had to overcome and at day ten we found ourselves on the brink of what I would soon consider to be the most disappointing, yet pleasantly revealing, experience of the trip.

After traveling for a mile or so with a homeless guy who we had met at a Kentucky Fried Chicken, we approached a monstrous bridge that would take us over an inlet and into a port-town. The homeless guy warned us about the town we were about to cross into and gave us some well-intentioned hotel advice for when we reached the backside of the bridge. We had tents, but safety was our first priority so spending a few bucks on a hotel was a reasonable compromise given the shady circumstances he had described.

Once we got over the bridge, we found out that the advised hotels were miles off our path and unrealistic for bedding that night. Other than the locations of the hotels, the guy from KFC was right – the town was terrible. The foul odors of burnt garbage hung in the air to let all who entered imagine – in the bad way – just what sort of experiences they could expect to encounter. On the first corner was a gas station that looked like it was waiting to be torn down, but to its misery the city developer would not pull the plug and it was forced to remain in a vegetative state that wouldn't even allow it to clean up its own soiled hind-parts. Adding to its character, the parking lot of this place was filled with every type of person one could imagine. There was a white-collar Mercedes' driver who was filling up his tank to ensure that he would have enough fuel to reach the far end of this dump before night-fall, a couple of port workers who were stopping by in their pick-up trucks to grab a prepackaged sandwich for dinner, and some homeless folks who lined the front of the store asking for spare change from everyone who entered and exited. Now, I am not one to go around assuming who is homeless and who is not based on spare change cups alone, but just so we're all clear, we did talk to several folks out front with cups and they informed us of their current living situation.

One woman, Maggie, in particular took a liking to us. For what seemed like an hour she told us her life story – the drugs, the prostitution, the shit town she was now forced to inhabit because of the cards she had been dealt. Or maybe it was the way she had played the cards? Either way, we listened intently. We laughed at those appropriate times when she would make a joke here and there poking fun at us or making up a satirical poem that fully captured the experience of that place. The poems were laced with colorful language and aimed to capture a sense of light-heartedness in a situation that was anything but lighthearted. And we would also empathize when she struggled through her personal stories of pain and of abuse wanting only to know that we would listen.

We all knew that we could not fix her situations, but then again I find that a rush to fixing a problem is often the last thing most people who are hurting need or want. In fact, I would argue that the people who are trying to help are the ones who want to rush to solutions because of their own discomfort with the situation. A quick fix for someone else's problem can get you out of their shit stained life a whole hell of a lot faster, but more than a quick fix I have found that people want compassion. They want others to sit – despite the discomfort – in their painful situations with them. They want people to fully engage with them where they are, not where the helping party wants them to be. Sure it's nice to talk up hallelujah stories with a person who *used* to be an addict or *used* to live on the street, but how often are we willing to just sit and meet a person in their current situation without trying to fix them like some sort of social or religious experiment? How often do we listen and not advise? Or perhaps the more important question to ask is why some privileged folks fail to grasp the humanizing nature an everyday conversation can have on a person?

After conversing with Maggie for quite sometime, it became apparent to all of us that the light of day was beginning to run short and that we would soon be walking the streets of a not-so-good area with no idea of where we were going or how long we would have to walk before we got there. Looking out for our best interest it was Maggie who took the lead. We stood on the corner with her waiting for the number six bus and when it finally arrived she pushed us onto the bus and told the driver where we were supposed to be dropped off. We rode that bus about two miles North and got dropped off at the figurative train tracks that ran through the middle of town. It was one of those places where the on and off ramps of the perpendicular interstate created a bridge that divided the adjoining towns by class and by race – the good from the bad.

Stepping off the bus, the driver pointed us in the direction of the "good" city's city hall and police station before making a left and circling back to towards the foul stench of burning garbage. Within ten minutes we had reached the city offices, but they had closed for the day. As luck would have it, across the street was one of those enormous mega-churches and size alone indicated that it surely had plenty of room inside for a few lonely vagabonds like us. Using my best CSI skills, I deduced that people must be inside by the looks of the scattered cars in the parking lot. We circled the building and found a side door propped open by a bag a sand. An untidy cut was slashed into its side and some of the contents had spilled onto the sidewalk.

Walking into the unlit gymnasium – presumably used for youth groups and basketball – we cautiously proceeded for fear that too much of a ruckus may turn away any potential help. The setting sun had difficulty pouring into the gymnasium through tinted doors, but our eyes quickly adjusted to the jarring darkness. Around the corner, there was a faint hint of artificial light and Rebecca and I decided to hold back while Kate approached what we would find out to be the kitchen. In the kitchen there stood a young white woman, probably 35 years old, who was packing leftovers into plastic shopping bags behind a twelve foot long stainless steel counter.

If I had to guess from the looks of her, her name was Jennifer. Her long, brunette hair and attractive features told me that she probably had a clean-cut husband, perhaps named Corey, with a strong jaw and made $55,000 a year selling something corporate. They probably met their junior year of college at an on-campus Bible study once the two of them were tired of all the binge drinking and random hook-ups. Giving their lives to Jesus, they remained celibate until their marriage, which was immediately after graduation and then they produced two children, James who was now 10 and played soccer and Sarah who was 7 and just as attractive as her mother exchanging brunette hair for blond. Jennifer wanted one more child, but Corey was worried that one more kid would cause a financial burden and put their yearly honeymoons to some arbitrary island to an abrupt stop. They would be divorced before Jennifer turned 40 due to Corey's infidelity. James would more or less follow in his father's footsteps.

I'm not actually 100 percent certain about all of the details of this fabricated family's aforementioned story, but it's as accurate as I can be going off a hunch.

Like performing surgery, Kate carefully announced her presence to Jennifer. In her best Christ-like manner Kate explained our situation and her family's life-long membership in the denomination. It was apparent that Jennifer was ever leery throughout the entire exchange, but finally Kate got bold and asked if the church could provide us with a place to stay. After all, the church was large and providing strangers a place to stay seemed pretty in-line with WWJD. We didn't require a lot of room or accommodations and I was content with simply bedding down on that gymnasium floor. Jennifer explained that she was not in a position to make such decisions, but that she would interject on our behalf to the head deaconess.

Kate returned to the other side of the gym where Rebecca and I had begun eavesdropping on Jennifer's telephone conversation. The eavesdropping wasn't completely on purpose, but what else were we suppose to do? Besides, the distance between Jennifer and us was small and the high ceilings caused her voice to echo.

"I know what your answer will be, but I told these kids I'd call."

A pause while the deaconess responded on the other end of the phone.

Jennifer continued, "Well, can you just come down here and tell them 'no' so that I don't have to bother with them?"

I could barely believe my ears! Wait, I take that back. I could believe my ears. It should be expected that a church so caught up in its own affairs would have little or no time to be bothered with three travelers who were clearly in need of a little compassion. At this point I wondered if they maybe had a stable out back with a manger that we could borrow.

When the deaconess did finally enter the gym she immediately began drilling us with questions that she already knew the answers to, but failed to comprehend because she chose not to acknowledge the circumstances right in front of her. She simply would not take our story of walking to raise awareness about sexual violence at face value. It may be hard to *imagine* that sort of circumstance (college students walking that far for so long does seem crazy), but I don't think it's too hard to *understand* that sort of circumstance (putting one foot in front of the other for a very long time). It was as if it was too much to ask her to exit her worldview and embrace other people's experiences and social actions as equally valid and important. I felt as if our purpose of walking to raise awareness about sexual violence was dismissed by her because our lifestyle didn't mesh with hers. We were somehow seen as unimportant because our thinking and our actions weren't in-line with her thinking and actions. Our means of social change may not have been as conventional or as contemporary as the ways in which the church goes about spreading their message nowadays, but it doesn't mean that what we were doing was less important. In fact, it could be argued that our idea of walking to spread a message of social change was inspired by the Bible. It wasn't, but it could be argued.

In the end, the deaconess was mean and dismissive. When we spoke, her eyes endlessly wondered around the darkened gymnasium like they were following the flight pattern of a fire-fly. When she spoke, she stared us down. Weaved throughout her pandering words were huffs and sighs. It was clear how much of a bother we had been to her day. Clearly, we were just one more hurdle between her cleaning up and her getting home. And when all was said and done, the hypocrisy was almost laughable. The leader of a church that preaches compassion, love, and hospitality was spitting in the face of the most perfect opportunity to practice these along with many other Biblical principles.

After the formalities of back and forth skepticism on both sides of the conversation, she finally agreed to let us sleep out back under the street lights. It wasn't the stable and manger that I had imagined, which in comparison to other options would have looked rather luxurious, but at least we had permission to camp on someone else's property until 7:00 am. The deaconess had informed us that we had to be gone by seven because that's the time when children would start arriving for school in the attached building. This was a fair enough request. You know, I don't mind looking out for the interests of curious children who would have questioned why there were three dirty people sleeping outside their classroom. Actually, the church could have used this situation as a good visual lesson for all those Bible stories. But regardless of the potential for childhood curiosity, what really got under my skin was the deaconess' tone. It simply reeked of what I would describe as condescending. With the conversation over we hoisted our packs onto our backs and began down the long hallway to the back door. Predictably, we did not get an escort.

It gets worse. We tried setting up our tent on the concrete afforded to us, but our tent was designed to anchor into a more earthy ground and without proper staking it just fell over in a partial collapse. Locked out, we had no access to restrooms to freshen up, brush our teeth, or use the toilet. Therefore, the act of relieving ourselves took place in a garden about ten feet from our tent in three feet tall brush and directly behind an eight-foot-tall statue of Jesus with open arms and a smile stretching across his Anglo-featured face. Given the painful realization that we had just been rudely turned away from the church, it was pleasant to know that at least Jesus would provide cover for our privates. Having read through the Bible, I presume that helping to cover my privates is something Jesus would do for me if I had to pee outside. He's rather compassionate like that.

The transition out of our walking clothes and into our pajamas – which were just clean shorts and a t-shirt – was speedy. It was joyous anytime we got a chance to shed the stench of the day and replace it with clean, non-sticky clothes. Almost immediately after pulling up my shorts a side door opened from inside the church – a different door from where we had exited – and suddenly an outpouring of a few dozen people filled our space. It was the choir.

"What do we have here?" exclaimed an older, balding gentleman in all of his holy-spirit filled excitement.

We gave him the brief, summarized, and memorized version of our mission statement. It just makes sense that after so many inquiries about our unusualness our response became quick, scripted, and automatic. Upon hearing this, a small group gathered around our make-shift living arrangements to hear more details about how we had come to be on their church's back patio.

Politely I said, "The deaconess said we could camp here for the night."

Ignorant of my true feelings towards that awful woman, all the saints became overjoyed with the church's hospitality. We continued the conversation by discussing some of our dilemmas with sleeping out back in terms of restrooms, the bugs, and the annoying street lights that would inevitably keep us up all night. But surprisingly, no one could think of a better solution. Apparently, no one there had a house either or even access to the bathrooms inside. Come to think of it, I'm not even sure any of them had an attention span because it was clear that they were not listening when they kept responding to us by talking about our eternal souls and handing us literature and magazines from right inside the church doors. Of course, this was literature and magazines that talked to Christian folks about how to serve in their daily lives and how to be more compassionate by meeting people's needs. Headlines such as *You Don't Have to Go on Missions to Be a Missionary* and *Love God by Helping Others* were visibly jumping off the pages. Yet, I suppose these folks were just like most other people who are sitting around waiting for someone else to take the initiative and carry the burden of responsibility to others.

Adding fuel to my angry fire that members of this particular church seemed to be burning, one man even told us to try and stay close to the canopy because it was suppose to rain.

"ARE YOU PEOPLE IDIOTS!?" I wanted to scream. But I didn't.

Here the three of us were; their free pass to everlasting life through serving some of their fellow humans in need and they missed it. Now I don't liken my self to sainthood nor do I think any charitable exceptions should have been made for our unique circumstances, but I do hope that I would have had enough sense to try and get some dirty kids who are walking to raise awareness about any social issue off of the concrete and out of the rain should the opportunity ever present itself. I understand the security issues involved, but for goodness sake, throw us in your garage! Plus, if you want to save someone's eternal soul, it may be a good idea to be a little more hospitable with the actions and a little less self-righteous with the literature.

After loading up our packs with literature – packs we had once already emptied of dead weight – the choir faded into the darkened parking lot and left us terrible, seemingly wretched souls in need of their literature on their crummy back patio. Currently, I am not trying to use the words "terrible" and "wretched" to be dramatic or even sarcastic. I seriously believe that they thought we were terrible and wretched heathens despite our confessions of faith and the fact that we were trying to practice compassion by walking the East Coast of America! They spoke to us as through we were categorically less than. Maybe it had to do with their disapproval over the co-ed living arrangements. Tired and worn, I sat upon a large rock and gazed into the night quietly watching the darkness as the final headlights of the choir's cars left the parking lot and disappeared behind the accumulating light mist that would soon bring the heavy rains.

We each had some quiet time that night before bed. For me, it was more like getting angry and getting sad time. I reflected on Maggie and overcome by the contradictions between her and the church people I could only laugh. Maggie had nothing and gave us everything. The church had everything and gave us nothing. The church had become so disconnected with the reality and concerns of everyday people that even Jesus left and had to be replaced by a stone statue replica. How perfectly fitting to his character that Jesus would run away from the church in order to reveal himself in the ill-infested corners of the world that smelled of burnt garbage? I remain deeply humbled knowing that the lessons *talked about* in the church are more oftentimes *lived out* by the folks rejected from the church. That message of understanding and compassion lived out by the addicts and the prostitutes so many of us try to avoid on our journey to reach the less righteous clergy in their beautiful buildings – only to be forced to sleep out in the rain.

# Not a Hero

**M**ore often than not, upon hearing about our how we walked the East Coast to raise awareness about sexual violence, people really begin to pile on the compliments of astounding proportion. In one instance I was even compared to the likes of Mahatma Gandhi.

Of course I find this comparison utterly absurd and would never hold my three month walk in comparison to a man who dedicated his life to non-violently fighting against British colonialism, but I do find it increasingly remarkable to  witness how we have become embodiments of iconic figures for so many folks both on the journey and back home. It's as if the big social justice dreams of various supporters were lived vicariously through us.

While I am continuously flattered and ever grateful for the support, I do however issue a word of caution for anyone who wishes to place our accomplishments above their earthly reality and human abilities. Furthermore, it is of my opinion that people should never place their role models on too high a pedestal for the fear that they may be tricked into thinking that they could never reach such heights themselves. When people become too entangled with distorted images of the messengers they lose sight of the message itself. Instead, people should use the energy generated by positive folks seeking to do positive things in an effort to create social change in their own communities. Everyone has the ability to evoke social change, but first one must clear their mind of idolized imagery that places other people's accomplishments out of reach. If we can stay focused on the message and not the people who carry that message, then we can truly begin to create our ideal communities. It is here that I think of the conscious momentum toward change that ordinary folks can partake in as everyday activism.

This next story is aimed at debunking any myth of my own sainthood as well as providing people with an alternative set of standards for defining what should be categorized as heroic.

Like any "well-adjusted" American male, I too give in to selfish temptation and enjoy my moments in the spotlight; feeling as if the world owes me something because of my great success without reflecting on any of the privileges and blessings afforded to me by the dominant culture that may have made it possible for me to succeed. Or at the very least, I sometimes don't recognize that dominant culture has made it nearly impossible for me to fail too miserably. Walking the East Coast was just one of those moments where I felt as if I had gotten everything right. I had put myself in a position of moral and ethical concern too great to be criticized by the vast majority of the criticizing public. In all honesty, who is going to disagree with us? Sexual violence is an issue that most everyone easily agrees on; the overwhelming opinion being that sexual violence is wrong. And because everyone agrees that it's wrong, it's hard to criticize a few college students who are walking the East Coast to raise awareness about it. In fact, the only flak we ever really received about the walk was in our methodological approach of walking on foot. We never got flak about the seriousness of the issue itself. Unfortunately, it was in these moments of overconfidence and "could do no wrong" attitude when I lost the most sight of what I was and who I was walking for.

If you one day decide to walk the Atlantic coast of Florida – or even just drive all 400 miles of it – you may become well informed as to how the highways and byways hug the coast never more than a few feet from the ocean. The smooth coastlines allow for this and I would guess that it is precisely this type of geographical perfection that makes traveling Highway 1 so appealing to bikers: both bikers with pedals and bikers with motors – we saw plenty of both. This pattern of smooth pavement with the coast in sight stays fairly much in place until the last 100 miles when the roads begin to travel more inland due to a rougher coastline. It was when we retreated inland on Highway 1 that I visibly noticed the staggering class change. Condos became trailers and fine dining became the greasy spoon. It does not surprise me that we still segregate ourselves along class-lines socially (how often do we talk to our friends who usually look like us about where we shop and how much our material goods cost?), but it does trouble me that the lines of real estate, class, and race are actually increasing their visibility.

Real estate is so blatant with its distaste for the poor that we have become desensitized to the absurd acts of discrimination. Neighbors are now living behind gated walls and people are only afforded the opportunity to find friends of a different class if they retreat online to a social network that most likely lists inaccurate information about a person in the first place. We can barely even borrow a cup of sugar from someone across the street because to get across the street and into a different neighborhood requires a picture ID and a security guard frisk. To some this may sound exaggerated, but I would challenge you to think about the last time you walked through a community that was visibly different from your own. And if you have, what did you *honestly* assume about the folks who lived there? During a time when not everyone had their own car, at least people were forced to walk through different parts of town and experience, if even for only a traveling moment, a different way of living. Now people can speed through these areas and in some cases can avoid them all together thanks to interstates. Poverty is easy to miss if you're never forced to live it or to look at it.

We stumbled upon one of these lesser known towns in Northern Florida. Being a few miles from the coast, I could see and smell and touch its unwantedness by tourists. I knew these people because their town was a lot like the town I was born in. The highway scrapped across the top of dirty gas stations – the only businesses that outsiders would touch on their way to more affluent people and things.

By the time we reached this town, we had a fairly set pattern as to how we liked to approach the day. We would be out of bed at sunrise ("bed" was quite a fluent concept by now), walking by 7:00 am, and trying to cover eight to ten miles before taking our first big break for lunch. After lunch and the occasional siesta, taken in the cool grass under the big palm leaves, we would walk six to seven more miles before dinner at roughly 5:00 pm. After dinner we would finish up the remaining three to four miles before looking for a place to bed down. When we reached this particular town on this particular day, it was 5:00 pm and time for dinner.

We approached the South end of town – the same end that we approached in every town – and quickly spotted one of those greasy spoons I mentioned earlier. Set just in front a trailer park, it blended into its landscape beautifully like a camouflaged G.I. sifting undetectably through the jungles of Vietnam. I entered slowly because I couldn't be bothered with rushing while I was admiring the plethora of lawn ornaments. Over-sized amphibians, wire flamingo sculptures, and vintage diner posters sucked you into the atmosphere. Now, when it comes to vintage posters on the outside of an old establishment like this, I often wonder if they were recently put up in the spirit of vintage decorating, or if they had in fact been there since the creation of the poster and management just forgot to take them down once they were outdated. Either way, the place had an inviting feel. Throwing our bags off to the side of the main entrance, which was a custom that many restaurants let us do and we were thankful for, we were seated by a very pleasant waitress.

"I saw y'all walking this morning on my way to work," she said in a very tender and welcoming voice. "That must have been about 15 miles back."

"Yeah, that was us." I tried to imitate her pleasantness. "We've been walking for a couple of weeks now all the way from Miami. We're walking to raise awareness about sexual violence."

With a warm smile, the waitress poured us some much needed water and retreated to the kitchen allowing us time to go over the menu.

As a way to conserve money and not over-indulge, the three of us often ordered just two meals and ate, what I like to call, "family style." The constant reaching over one another and passing plates around the table does something to bring a group of folks closer together. I suppose it helped us break out of the individualized identity that comes with the labeling of "my fork," "my spoon," "my beef," "my broccoli."

It's amazing how the quiet act of eating from one another's plate allows you to enter into one another's life on a more personal level.

Having collectively decided on our order, Kate retreated to the restroom to wash up. The task of washing up in a restaurant restroom usually took about fifteen minutes and until this trip I had never literally washed my arms up to my elbows nor had I engaged in the act of washing my face and drenching myself in sunscreen just before eating at a public establishment. By now it was something I did on a frequent basis. It had become, as they say, habit forming.

When Kate was gone, the waitress returned with two pitchers of water and that same warm smile. She flipped open her order booklet and pulled a pencil from behind her ear.

Rebecca smiled at her, glancing back and forth from the menu, and said, "Well have the chicken dinner and a turkey sandwich. And I know it says you charge extra for splitting up meals, but we were wondering if you could waive that?"

"No problem. What are you all doing again?"

"We're walking to raise awareness about sexual violence."

I watched as those words enter into the waitress' soul and her mood became calmer than it had already been – more somber. Her voice lowered to just above a whisper and I knew what I was about to hear before the first words even emptied over her thin, red lips. Then she began.

"I'm not originally from here. In fact, I've only been here a few months."

She sighed and collected herself. Rebecca and I briefly stole a look at one another.

"Yeah, back in Montana, my 14 year old daughter was raped two years ago. I put her into counseling, but it wasn't working so finally one day we packed up and moved out here so she could be in a better space mentally."

With that, she raised her head and a slight smile came across her face, her eyes piercing through to my heart. Then she nodded and returned to the kitchen. It was in this moment that the walk for me was forever changed. I was less than three weeks in and already I had found myself realigning my priorities. Through ten months of planning, the three of us struggled both internally and externally with issues regarding how to get this walk going for *us*. People would join *our* cause determined to walk with us and then bail unsympathetic to the fact that their abandonment had cost us time and money. Yes, we traveled around central Michigan looking for supporters. Yes, we invested our own time and money into propagating our "adventure of a lifetime." And, yes, I was set in knowing that this walk was to going to change the way people think about the issue of sexual violence.

However, the unconnected hands of financial and media support are trivial if they are tainted by uncompassionate advocates who parade *their* social issues around as if they are somehow in ownership over the struggle that so many marginalized and forgotten people deal with on a daily basis. But with that waitress's nod, all of my priorities for this walk changed and I was reminded why I had begun advocating against sexual violence in the first place. With that nod, the waitress reminded me of who I was really trying to gain the support of. I was walking to gain the support of survivors. With that nod, I was reminded that while our faces may be plastered in newspapers and on the nightly news for the "heroic" task set before us, we were not heroes and it was not our faces that represented the issue of sexual violence. If we need to have heroes, then the heroes should be the everyday faces of those affected by sexual violence. The faces of our neighbors, our friends, and our loved ones who have been rendered faceless and their voices rendered voiceless and yet despite the overwhelmingly emotionless shrug of society's indifference they continue to survive. These invisible attributes are what represent the issue.

This single mom packed up the last 40 years of her life's work and moved from one coast to another where she knew no one only to find herself living in a trailer park and waitressing at a greasy diner so that her little girl could have a chance at reclaiming the peace of mind that was violently taken from her. *She* was a hero.

By comparison, the three of us were concerned and responsible college students who wanted to do what we could to help bring attention to the issue of sexual violence. And what we did was important. Yet the journey we freely chose to embark on is far different than what may be coercively or forcefully chosen for someone else. Sure it can be said that we unselfishly gave up three months of our early 20s to do something admirable. To some extent, I would agree. But what we – and I mean all advocates – often lose sight of is that for every piece of hell we hear about on our journeys as advocates, others live this struggle everyday. This is not to discount survivors of sexual violence who are also advocates, but it is to say that although we gave up three months, this waitress had to alter her entire life. There are *choices* in advocacy work.

Additionally, and as a point of perspective, we should be mindful in not confusing her actions as something unique. As remarkable as her move was, I quickly discovered through more and more interactions with everyday folks along the way that heroic feats like this were a common thread that weave together the stories of people affected by sexual violence. What's heartbreaking is that this waitress' story *wasn't* extraordinary. What's heartbreaking is that this waitress' story is all too ordinary.

Kate returned from the restroom and it was obvious that the mood of table had changed. Respecting the privacy of the waitress, Rebecca and I never told Kate what had happened. And being the understanding and respectful person she is, Kate never asked. When our meal was over, we kindly asked the waitress for our check. However, instead of presenting us a bill, she presented us with $15.

"I told the others what ya'll were doing and we pulled some money together. It ain't much, but it's all we got."

Aware of the visibly desperate financial conditions of the area, we politely tried to decline, but the waitresses would have no word of it. They wouldn't let us pay our bill nor would they accept our smart-ass attempt at leaving a $15 tip. Walking out the door to be greeted by the setting sun, the circumstances that unfolded at the diner that evening are what I thought about the rest of the night, the rest of the trip, and what I continue to think about today. What we did when we walked the East Coast of America was important, creative, unique, and possibly a little crazy, but by no means was it heroic or worthy of iconic praise. To this day it remains important that we continue to spread the word and educate others about the social injustice of sexual violence through our daily choices, but anything I do can never be categorized as something more important than what countless others do for the cause everyday. Nor can it be categorized as anything more important than what you can choose to do for the cause today.

Please embrace the message tighter than you embrace the messenger. And in that process of advocacy, never forget that we need to mindfully navigate the terrain of speaking *with* people who have been deemed too culturally unimportant to make a ripple in the consciousness of humanity. We must be careful to never speak *for* them. Finally, we should remember that the true heroes in the fight against sexual violence are like the waitress we met in Northern Florida. They are people who are willing to give up their lives in order to help people they love through the everyday struggle. No, we're not heroes for walking. The three of us are just fortunate in different ways for being blessed with the opportunity of having been touched by the lives of heroes.

# Good Fun, Good Food, Good Friends

**B**efore we left Florida, we had to make a quick stop in the self-proclaimed "oldest town" in America. Now, I am unsure of how one goes about claiming the title of America's "oldest town," but it seems fairly far fetched to proclaim "oldest town" when people have been living within the territory of what we now know as the United States of America for several and possibly even hundreds of generations before anyone signed a deed and thus proclaimed the territory of St. Augustine an official town. But I suppose it would be the Western thing to do in proclaiming official discovery and occupancy of something when and only when white people arrived. It kind of reminds me of that Zen koan about a tree falling in the woods when nobody's around to hear it: "If a territory is occupied, but there are no white people there to document it, does it really exist?"

Another small bit of history that fascinated me about St. Augustine was the stark contrast in the name of the town and its racial history. Being the "oldest town" in America during a time of rampant slave trade, any grammar school child could guess that the city's history is packed, and some may even refer to it as tainted, with slave remembrance. While the slavery that existed in St. Augustine and the race riots that succeeded in the 1900s were far from uncommon – especially in the segregated South – what was completely astonishing to me was finding out that the town of St. Augustine, Florida is named after an Algerian saint. However, I suppose that this naming should come as little surprise to me and somehow it actually makes sense that the identity confused history of America would name its original city and first slavery capitol after a revered, admired, and worshiped black man from Africa. The quizzical look I gained at the time of learning this rather interesting and seemingly paradoxical historical fact would soon melt off my face as I freely enjoyed the nostalgic atmosphere of the famous, yet historically ironic, city of St. Augustine.

We reached the city by bridge and, as if they had been waiting for our deliverance on the other side, were greeted by a group of war protesters. Because the last few years of my life has been spent around plenty of idealistic college kids (me being one of them) who were anxious to voice any opinion contradictory to that of their traditional parents, war protesters and vegetarians don't tend to heighten my interests too rapidly. But these protesters were different. These war protesters were veterans and not just any veterans. They were veterans who had *voluntarily* joined the military back in their youth and had fought in a few different wars; not just the unpopular ones. We immediately hit it off with them and even held their "Honk Against the War" signs for a minute or two. After a few pictures and exchanges of hope for each other's success, we continued our little journey into the colonial past.

St. Augustine is a lot like any other colonial town you would find up North and the experience was complete with tacky t-shirts and even tackier costumes covering the sweaty bodies of those portraying British and American troops. Sometimes I question the authenticity of these costumes. I mean, did the armies of the sixteen and seventeen hundreds not have any clothes that were better suited for the humid Florida summers? My grappling with questions such as this soon passed and we quickly grew bored with the cobblestone streets lined with shops where we could purchase those little Dixie cannon magnets with our names on them. We decided that it would be best to find a more relaxing way to enjoy the city.

On the North end of the historic district we found a small information center with a very pleasant woman inside. We asked her for information about cheap entertainment and also inquired about the availability of an inexpensive hotel. As she began to dial a few local tourist spots, we dropped our packs and explored what few artifacts they had in the information center pertaining to the city's history. From memory, there were two themes on exhibit: theatre entertainment and trains. My guess is that these themes are most likely a staple to any good tourist town history. What city didn't have a theatre and a train station back in the day? After several minutes on the phone, she called us back together from the various locations we had scattered off to and I could never have imagined what she was about say:

"I made a few phone calls and was able to get you VIP city passes and train tickets."

I gathered up my jaw that had dropped to the ground and we all hastened to stammer out a shocked, "Thank you!"

The VIP passes she managed to swindle for us basically meant that we could get into the Ripley's Believe It or Not Museum across the street. The train tickets were for the sight-seeing trolley that took folks on a history lesson ride through downtown. Gathering up the details along with a few tourist maps, we thanked the woman repeatedly and headed out front just in time to hop on a trolley that was just pulling into the station.

The trolley ride wasn't overly exciting. In fact, I'm pretty sure that all three of us dozed on and off throughout the trip. That's not to say that I'm ungrateful or that the ride was worthless. After all, the trolley ride did provide us an hour of rest that kept us off our feet and under some shade. Even though other people were getting on and off at numerous "destination" points, we stayed on until the trolley made a complete circle around the city to where it had originally picked us up. Rested, we gathered our things, exited the trolley, and rushed over to the Ripley's Believe It or Not Museum.

If you have never been, the Ripley's Believe It or Not Museum is an absolutely remarkable place and I highly recommend it as a destination point for anyone looking for a fun-filled vacation. I know that sometimes the exhibits may be interpreted as corny or tacky, but on the whole I think the Ripley's movement has a lot to teach us about motivation, perseverance, and creativity. Having the world's longest nose hair or riding a unicycle across the country backwards may seem like a waste of time, but I'm not going to fault someone for dreaming up an idea and tirelessly following through with it. Shoot, those same folks that grace the walls of Ripley's probably think it's equally wasteful and *exponentially more ridiculous* that some people would spend 30 years in front of a computer doing mind-numbing work that they hate in an attempt to satisfy people they probably dislike more than their job. At least the folks at Ripley's are trying to be a little bit more creative with how they make a living, and they're being remembered for achieving a goal they set out to accomplish.

Needless to say, I enjoyed my time at the Ripley's Believe It or Not Museum in St. Augustine, Florida. Besides the fact that I got to learn about the histories of artistic people doing what they loved, the overall atmosphere of the museum was also just crazy enough to make me feel like what we were doing was somewhat normal. Additionally, it gave me hope that maybe one day I'll get the honor of being included in one of these museums. I've already come up with a few ideas, which include copying the Bible onto a roll of toilet paper (maybe two, the Bible is pretty long) and creating an entire house out of some arbitrary junk yard item like soda bottles or used tires. Whatever direction this whole thing goes, I hope Superman and that woman from *Baywatch* show up on my doorstep during the final moments of completion.

After a wonderful and restful night in our inexpensive hotel room made possible by the generous woman who gave us every discount there was because she found our journey encouraging, we headed North the following day on what may have been the hottest, most humid day thus far. What made it worse was the lack of rest stops North of St. Augustine. It almost felt like we were walking on a treadmill – our feet kept moving and we weren't going anywhere. We made it maybe eight miles when we finally found a little English pub off the road, hidden behind some shrubbery. Not knowing when or where the next oasis was going to be, we all agreed that we were going to take full advantage of this stop for however long we needed to.

Following the cobblestone pathway through a small vine covered pergola, we reached an outdoor patio where two men and a woman were lifting their glasses and chattering merrily.

"Where did you all come from?" the older man said with a hint of witty sarcasm.

We playfully jousted back, explaining our story and asking how the food was inside.

"Oh, this place!" His voice shrunk to a whisper as if trying to tell us classified information. "This is one of those hidden secrets that not too many folks know about. But it's got some great food and spirits…if you're into that sort of thing."

Before long, we had learned that the younger man and woman were together and they were the ones who would eventually lead us inside the pub. As for the older man, he seemed to be in a rush and soon said goodbye only to begin cutting his way through the back field. Apparently he lived over there, but all I could see was a quarter mile of meadow that ended at a wall of trees. I don't know. Maybe he lived with those guys in the commercials who make cookies inside of their tree-houses. It wouldn't have surprised me.

Inside, the pub was exactly how I would have imagined an English pub to be. Various flags from all over Europe were hung from the darkened wood walls and ceiling. The translucent, yellow-tinted windows gave the place a shadowy, yet inviting, feel. The young couple, who didn't work there but treated the place like it was a part of their soul, sat us down in a booth near the front of the pub. The deep-brown leather was riveted into the aged wood and stuck to my sweaty legs as I attempted to scoot around the circular table.

"Get whatever you want. I'm buying," said the man who had led us inside.

He and his partner were so friendly that we didn't even bother with formal introductions. But then again, formal introductions usually serve comfort rather than the interest of really getting to know a person. Asking someone's name seems to be just a way to fill silence in a new setting when you have nothing more interesting to lead off a conversation with. With these two, it was almost like our conversation was so good that we didn't want to interrupt it with arbitrary questions of personal labels. However, through meaningful conversation we later found out that his name was Jay and her name was Mira.

Sitting in that sticky leather booth all I wanted was some water as well as some fish and chips. Can you really blame me though? Given the current atmosphere, I just had to succumb to the cultural delicacy pressures that were surrounding my taste buds – "when in Rome." Kate and Rebecca also gave into Rome and decided to drink down a couple of brews in order to really soak up their surroundings. You know, it's funny; despite Kate being underage for the first half of the trip, people never carded her or any of us until after her 21st birthday.

Jay and Mira stayed at the bar and gave us some space as we ransacked through our meal. When we were done, Jay picked up the tab and asked us what our plans were for the rest of the day.

"Seriously?" I mocked sarcastically. "We're walking up the East Coast."

There was a pause and Jay's face read blank.

"That's all we do," I searched his face for understanding and my tone became dry and deliberate, "everyday," I added for clarity.

There was another pause and finally I offered again.

"We're walking."

In his contagious form, Jay began laughing. He had one of those big belly laughs like Santa Claus and soon we all joined in. I wasn't quite sure what we were all laughing about, but like I said, Jay's spirit was contagious. And much like the Holy Ghost, when Jay's spirit moved, it moved us too.

"Well, we're going down to St. Augustine for a Reggae Fest on the docks," Jay said. "Afterwards, you're more than welcome to stay at my place."

Jay's hospitality was a double-edge sword and it cut deep. The thought of Reggae music and a bed to sleep in that night was oh so tempting, but in order to do so we had to sit in a car for ten minutes and torturously relive the miles it took us all morning to conquer. It was a painful conundrum, but we eventually decided that a Reggae party was too tempting to pass up. Plus, we needed to take a little time now and again to enjoy ourselves. After stuffing the packs into his trunk and stuffing ourselves into his back seat, I rested my head against the window and closed my eyes for the trip back choosing to ignore the painful reality of traveling South.

The Reggae music on the dock that afternoon was a delicious treat. More importantly, and rather unexpectedly, it also offered us the opportunity to talk to lots of folks about what we were doing.

Even though there were far more exciting things going on within the parameters of the dock, it seemed as if an unusual amount of people flocked our way to see what all the hype was about. I like to imagine that it had something to do with those matching teal shirts that stuck out against the backdrop of cool, casual club wear. Nonetheless, our mission was to generate conversation about sexual violence and this atmosphere provided that type of circumstance.

After about two hours of mingling on the dock, we headed back in the direction of the pub. Mira had to get back home in time for her ex-husband to drop off her eight year old son Cody. Traveling nearly 100 miles per hour down the highway, we made it back to her condo just as Cody was exiting his father's car. In light of Cody's visible confusion as to who the hell we were, the six of us clamored into Mira's place.

Once inside, the conversation got interesting. For us, having a conversation with an eight year about what we were doing was a bit trying and required some creative effort. Naturally, kids enjoy asking you a bunch of question about who you are and why you're carrying everything you own on your backs for an entire summer, but to get into the specifics of raising awareness about sexual violence isn't always age appropriate. Therefore, anytime we met a younger person we always looked toward their parents to take the lead. Sure it was a copout of sorts, but I'm not taking the heat if the information I perceive as appropriate is miles beyond what a kid's parents think is appropriate. So we slowly and clumsily wrestled through the first part of the conversation with Cody trying to take cues from the way Mira moved her eyes or nodded her head. Using this Morse code like technique, we soon took on a persona similar to people who try to help the police catch bad guys. Not entirely accurate, but close enough to pacify the imagination of an eight year old.

Hanging out with Jay, Mira, and Cody that afternoon was obnoxiously fun. First, a wrestling match between Cody and Rebecca ended with spilling Jay's glass of red wine on the white carpet. But to my surprise, nobody really freaked out. Sure it became a mad rush to the kitchen for paper towels and Cody had a blast filling up countless jars of water as he got to throw them all over the carpet, but it sort of turned into a crazy game instead of panicked catastrophe. In my assessment, Mira was more concerned about her son having fun than yelling at him for an accident. (Plus, I think it was really more Rebecca's fault anyway).

After the wine incident, which by the way we did successfully manage to get out of the carpet, Jay, Cody, and I quickly found ourselves outside playing a pickup game of football on the golf course that stretched through Mira's backyard. After about 30 minutes of pitch and catch, the ladies joined us outside and it soon became a two-hand touch game between the heated rivalry of men verses women. Given the history between the two teams, I should have guessed that the game would play on for a lot longer than it needed to and that it would actually become quite exhausting. Seriously though, what drives people to be so competitive over gender-sided football games? I think the dynamics of this rivalry is indicative of some sort of cultural problem. I'm just glad that I don't give into this petty cultural debate between the battle-of-the-sexes and that I can say without malicious intent that, in the end, the guys won by a couple of touchdowns. Although Jay did comfort Mira by lying to her and telling her that the victory was hers. Unlike the rest of us competitive junkies, she wasn't really paying attention to the score and wouldn't have noticed the difference either way.

We went inside as the sun was setting and the temperature began to turn cool. I was under the impression that we would just order a couple of pizzas or something cheap for dinner, but Jay and Mira had other plans. Rummaging through the phone book, they found the address of a posh restaurant and we left with little knowledge of where we were going.

When we finally arrived inside the place, I was in awe of how elegant it was and how disastrous I looked as I was unshaven and still wearing my dirty teal shirt and dusty shorts. I had always heard fantasy-like stories of places like this where the cooks entertain the guest while preparing their meals right in front of them around an oversized hot griddle, but up until now I had never actually seen the inside of a Japanese steak house. For some, this may seem like an everyday experience and my bewilderment an unnecessary exaggeration, but I ask you to accept the reality that I come from a family background where $30 a plate dinners are something that only exist in kingdoms and Hollywood.

While scanning over the menu, I acted as if I knew what I was doing. To me, reading the menu at a Japanese steak house was similar to reading a "choose your own adventure" book. A small anecdote of information was placed before you and you were responsible for mixing and matching the ingredients. One wrong choice and you were dead – or simply unsatisfied with the order. Mumbling to myself and trying rather unsuccessfully to pronounce the surplus of different dishes, it soon become apparent to Jay and Mira that I was only reading the less expensive items for fear of running up too high a bill. With no shame and zero censorship, Jay boastfully proclaimed a Jubilee like celebration where the three of us were commanded to order the best food options provided by the menu and to pay no mind to the extravagant prices because he would be picking up the bill.

With an air of thankfulness that caused me to tearfully well up on the inside without giving away my vulnerability on the outside, I humbly proceeded to find a few menu items that looked both appetizing and familiar. Along with our food, Jay ordered a few rounds of Sake. Soon we were all yelling, "Kung-Pow" and I graciously swallowed down a couple of shots despite my adverse reaction to the warm, bitter liquor. After experiencing the street-like performance by our chef and stuffing myself full of rice, vegetables, and a variety of different types of seafood, I was more than elated with how the whole day had turned out.

Jay dropped off Mira and Cody back at their place, but it took a good 30 minutes of appreciation and good-byes before we left. As we all stood there in the parking lot of Mira's condo, I calculated the probability of meeting up with strangers at lunch only to spend the next ten hours with them where both parties have an attitude of openness and submersion (I also calculated the amount of cash they had just dropped on us, which I figured to be about $300. If Jay or Mira are reading this, we are eternally grateful). Sharing and embracing our last moments of fellowship, we playfully watched Cody run up and down the length of the parking lot while wearing one of our packs. He had been making plans all evening about coming with us and was now illustrating to us how physical able he was.

We finally gave Mira and Cody one last hug before crawling back into Jay's car. We were going to stay at his place because it was closer to our route. Although it was painful to say good-bye, the three of them helped me realize for the first time in my life how important friendships really are. Our walk was a journey of brief encounters and on a big enough timeline, that's all life really is. I had been walking in and out of other peoples' lives for my entire life, but this friendship with Jay, Mira, and Cody broke it down to a more manageable level. You see, with the three of them I knew that our time was coming to a close the moment we said hello to one another. So I made sure I did everything I could to enjoy my time with them and let them know how much I appreciated them. However, what seems to be my downfall in other relationships is that I think I have all the time in the world and I never allow myself to feel that sense of urgency and therefore, never exhaust myself in expressing love and appreciation.

I feel that this same concept is true with advocacy work. Too often advocates get caught up in the details of perfection and allow great opportunities for proactive resistance to slip by. I don't know how much longer I will be able to fully devote myself to the issue of raising awareness about sexual violence, but I must always remember that my time in finite. We should all begin making proactive choices *everyday* that will impact the movement to end sexual violence because we never know when those opportunities will present themselves again.

Since that night, I have yet to reconnect with Jay, Mira, and Cody and chances are good I may never reconnect with them. But I can tell you this; the love and acceptance they showed me during that one moment in time is something we could all learn a lot from. I hope to remember and share that kind of love with all of those who surround my life everyday because, on a long enough timeline, one of those days will be our last encounter.

# Disney is Destroying the World with Good Intentions

**L**eaving Florida was difficult. Not in the emotional, "Oh Florida I've spent so much time with you now I never want to leave you," sort of way. But in the, "Are you serious! Why are there so many highways and cross roads through Jacksonville that I can't find my out," sort of way. Sure, if we were in a car we could just take the interstate all willy-nilly never paying any mind to the difficulty of traveling the back-roads by foot. Although traveling the back-roads of Northern Florida did have its perk. Its one and only bloody perk. But I was in no position to be picky about my perks, so I took them gratefully with a smile on my face.

The difficulty we knew we had to face by following the coast of Florida was that when we got to Northern Florida we literally fell into the ocean. All of the back roads and highways stopped and the only way to get across by foot was to detour west for who knows how far. We were in no mood for taking detours and I was more inclined to swim up the coast as opposed to unnecessary backtracking. Thankfully, Jay lived close enough to the Georgia border to know the ins and outs of border shortcuts.

Before we went to bed that night at Jay's, Jay drew us a map on the back of a coffee stained piece of discarded paper that he found in his trash can. It reeked of stale citrus, but I suppose it wasn't any more rank than the clothes we had on. What he drew out for us were directions to a ferry that crossed a mile wide channel that would lead us right into Jacksonville without having to detour for what may have been two extra days of walking. This was perfect! Not only we were going to save time and extra walking, but I was going to get that perk and fulfill one of my goals for the trip – riding on a boat.

Up until now there were very few goals for the trip. Mainly it was the straight forward objective of raising awareness about sexual violence. But as the days wore on and turned into weeks, which ultimately turned into mind-numbing forgetfulness of time and location, I had to come up with fun little games to play in order to pass the time. One of those games was setting up a few goals for the trip that would seem like major achievements for any travelers who needed to entertain themselves as the pavement wore on and on. I can't remember all of the successfully completed goals I set since I failed to write them down, but as mentioned, one of those goals was riding in a boat. There were also some goals I didn't achieve such as riding in an eighteen-wheeler and meeting Morgan Freeman. I know, meeting Morgan Freeman seems like a lofty goal, but I figured that he lived in the South and with a little publicity we may have been able to pull it off. And just in case Morgan Freedom is reading this, I'd still like a chance to reach my goal.

After the ferry ride across the channel, which cost $1 for each standing passenger, we made our way through Northern Jacksonville and into the small town of Pawnee, Florida. Pawnee was a nice little suburbia town just outside the concrete jungle of Jacksonville and gave me that rush of relaxation I feel when a congested interstate of backed-up traffic finally opens up and I can start traveling 70 mile per hour again. Jacksonville was stifling and I was longing to sit in a shady place away from the oppressing sun and the hot blacktop that had been reflecting heat up my calves all day.

On the South side of Pawnee sat a small little church. It was one of those hip-looking churches with modern architecture and bright signs that read like catchy pop-culture: "Are you going to accept this sin? *Deal or No Deal*" and "Jesus is coming. Will you be a *Survivor*?" When did the appropriation of crappy music and reality television become the "it" thing for contemporary Christianity? I thought the church was supposed to offer something we couldn't get by watching our average four hours of television a day.

Despite my cynicism and skepticism, the folks at the church were very warm and welcoming once they finally answered the door. We must have circled that place three times and knocked on every tinted window and door that we couldn't see into before someone finally answered! Once inside, a "cool" pastor, Pastor Jeff, greeted us with his bright Hawaiian shirt, tight fitting blue-jeans, and goatee that screamed, "You can be a hipster and still love Jesus! I am!" And he was.

We started chatting about what we were doing and where we had been. To Pastor Jeff, everything we said was "Great!" and "Awesome!" His wide eyes and endless smiling made me feel like we were the most important thing he had come across all day. Although I can't help but think that if his demeanor would have been like this after the sun had gone down I would have been horrified and completely freaked-out. Seriously, how happy can one person be for any length of time?

Anyway, Pastor Jeff quickly showed us around before passing us off to some eight or nine college interns who were suppose to make us feel more comfortable as "peers." They grabbed our bags like we had just checked-in to the Hyatt and took us to the game room where we would be able to sleep later that night. Walking back into the youth church, which was a basketball court and folding chairs, we made a circle near the sound equipment and started talking to the interns about sexual violence.

To my surprise, they were genuinely interested in our mission and had an enormous amount of questions to ask about the subject.

"Is it really a big problem?"

"Yeah, one in four women will be assaulted in her lifetime."

"What about women who lie about it?"

"Well, actually it's only about four percent, which is the same false report rate for any other violent crime."

"How can I help people?"

"Just listen and believe. Too many people don't believe and then survivors don't want to report."

This question and answer period went on like this for about an hour. There was even a guy talking about trying to do some of his own advocating at his college. I don't know if he ever got anything off the ground, but the fact that people were talking about the issue and becoming genuinely concerned made me happy.

Kate, Rebecca, and I eventually retreated to the game room for dinner, which consisted of some deli products from the local Kroger a block up the road, and then got some rest before the church events got going that night. I believe it was a Wednesday night, but either way, it was a youth group night. This meant lots of kids and lots of noise.

I always liked the idea of youth group nights at churches. Even if you don't necessarily believe in all the Jesus lessons they throw in during a 15 minute service at the end of all the chaos, it's hard to argue that there's any harm in giving kids a positive environment to play sports, make crafts, and be around high school mentors for a couple of hours every week. Yet, this particular night caused me a huge amount of struggle. A struggle that I'm still wrestling with almost a year later.

What I'm about to disclose next will, without a doubt, cause a chain reaction of confusion, tension, and hateful scorn. But in the interest of being real, it's important that I share. To get right to it, I was somewhat misleading when I skimmed over the details of the youth group. My incomplete account wasn't meant to be fraudulent, but simply to illustrate how misinformed I had originally been with the entire situation myself. When I heard, "there's a youth group meeting tonight," I assumed that the children of the adult members of the church were going to be the ones coming in to participate in all of the aforementioned activities. What I failed to realize was that the youth group being held tonight was a youth group that consisted *only* of kids who were bused in from inner-city Jacksonville.

If you have failed to grasp the complete picture of this situation, please allow me to rephrase so that you can fully understand the weight of the previous statement.

The youth group to be held on this evening was a separate – some may even say segregated (I would say segregated) – youth group that consisted *only* of inner-city black kids. My assumption is that the white kids of suburbia, the white kids whose parents actually attended this church, had their youth group meetings on some other night.

Now some folks don't like to hear the reality of the situation, especially those who put on events like this. But the truth is the truth no matter how innocent one's intentions may be. As an outsider visiting the church, all I saw that night was a white church busing in black kids to provide them a positive environment in which to indoctrinate them with religion. I understand the argument that, "God doesn't see color," but from where I was standing, no one in that room was God and if anyone failed to see the deep contrast between skin tones, then they were either legally blind or wholly ignorant.

The arguments for busing in black kids (some like to use a less loaded term like "urban kids," but urban is just a colorblind word for black) from bad neighborhoods to teach them how to be upstanding Christians is rooted in good intentions, but to do so without acknowledging the potential for detrimental effects is just irresponsible. For one, what kind of message do white folks send to young black kids when they *physically* take them to a "better" neighborhood to interact *only* with positive white mentors? Furthermore, if the church is going to get a hold of some college interns, why can't they recruit more people of color so that the young folks are exposed to people who look like them?

If we keep operating our youth services from a white-centered, white-owned, white-helper viewpoint, we do nothing more than perpetuate the worldview that white is good and black is bad. That's why the whole idea of "diversity" is so important. Diversity shouldn't be about tokenizing certain folks to fill a quota in your company, but instead should be about offering different perspectives of whom and what people can be.

To make matters worse, the service message at this particular youth night was presented by a married white couple who had been motivational speakers at Jesus rallies for almost a decade. The husband was a strong man who wore a shirt that read, "Built Lord Tough." Here was that pop-culture appropriation again. This guy was enormous and the bulk (no pun intended) of his act consisted of bending steel rods and giving the obvious anecdote about how Jesus gives you the strength to do anything. After he military pressed a couple of kids and twirled them around like helicopters, he closed by bending some rebar with his teeth. Apparently, Jesus is also in the business of selling super strength toothpaste.

All in all, I was okay with this guy and his message about being strong in character and how he conveyed this message to the kids by illustrating his physical strength. I have been told that kids need those visual messages to accompany the deeper meanings of things. In fact, I was actually kind of impressed with his vein covered biceps as they bulged and contorted while he twisted the metals in a superfluous manner. What infuriated me was the follow up message delivered by his beautiful wife.

Let me begin by mentioning that she was gorgeous! In perfect alignment with dominant ideologies pertaining to beauty and gender, she was tall with a slim build and long brunette hair. This was all complimented nicely by her shiny white teeth that were well positioned in a permanent smile. Throughout her husband's performance, I just thought she was there as an assistant – someone needs to keep track of all that metal – but as soon as her husband retreated into the kitchen to ice down his depleted muscles she dove right into her own testimony. In short, her testimony focused on the fact she was a former Disney princess, which of course made perfect sense to me. She had worked all over the country and traveled to various parts of the world playing everyone from Snow White to Belle in *Beauty and the Beast*. Now she was hitting up the youth circuit telling little girls that they were beautiful and that they could be anything they wanted to be when they grew up including a Disney princess.

This is when I, from the back row, lost it. I didn't lose it overtly, but rather through a violent whisper to Rebecca who was sitting next to me. Don't get me wrong, I think all kids should be told that they are beautiful and that they can be whatever they want to be, but having some white woman telling little black girls that they could be Disney princesses just seemed irresponsible. Not because little black girls don't deserve positive representation among Disney princesses, but rather because there's no representation for little black girls to look to. More pointedly, has she ever taken a good look at her profession? What white princess were these girls suppose to look up to for inspiration? Who is the black Disney princess role model for these girls from Jacksonville? Quite frankly, I think this woman's time would have be better spent using her connections to the Disney monopoly to try and get them to create more positive representations – or really, any representations – of black people in their children's cartoon movies. But then again, that battle may prove to be more difficult than I realize seeing that Disney couldn't even depict black people in Africa when they recently remade *The Lion King* and *Tarzan*.

Critically picking apart the racial representation of Disney in this fashion makes some white folks defensive. However, while I understand the arguments for "colorblindness" and would like to believe that children don't categorize based on color, I can't ignore that colorblind stances are easy for white people to take when they have such a vast amount of role models to choose from. Not to mention the fact that adults still categorize based on color so it's logical for me to assume that these mental categorizations probably had something to do with our racialized childhoods. It has been long established, particularly by people of color, that dominant society continuously shows white people as princesses and princes, teachers and doctors, lawyers and congressmen.

By comparison, black children's options and the options of other racial minorities for positive representation are severely limited in mass communication. To keep it real, when most black children look for themselves on television or in magazines, they are exposed to a proportionally higher number of rappers and athletes over intellectuals, professional folks, and yes, even princesses. It would be quite bold of a white parent to claim that they would be completely unresponsive if their little white children were disproportionately exposed to media that depicted them as country music artists and hockey players while black and brown people flooded the rest of their television stations like a BET takeover (which, by the way, is owned by white people and offers up a great conversation about *who* is making the decisions about *what* black people can look like on a television station supposedly created for black folks).

In addition, the images black children see of themselves are also at the mercy of sexual violence educators. As racialized representations relate to the issue of sexual violence, what I continually find problematic in the field is how sexual violence educators reproduce racism while at the same time trying to alleviate sexism. This is often done by using a disproportionate amount of images from hip-hop and rap videos that depict black men being hyper-sexual, hyper-violent, and hyper-unintelligent.

While these images should be deconstructed and the artists should be held accountable for the role they play in perpetuating violence against women, black artists should be no more the scapegoat for cultural sexism than the representations we see in white country music or the discriminatory gendered practices perpetuated by corporate white male capitalist. In truth, sexual violence educators deconstruct

xually violent because it's more overt and this
ut we as educators cannot allow our laziness to
;es of more subtle sexism become an excuse for
n we only succeed in labeling black men as the
violence.

ink any of these white folks at the church
... intended and they most likely had genuine concerns about
the harsh circumstances that often surround young black children
in urban areas. What scares me is the lack of critical reflection that
would require even people with the best intentions to look at the
reality of the situation for what it is: black kids being bused out to
white mentors. Instead of placing these children into environments
that solicit suburbia assimilation, it may be more admirable for the
white church to start demanding some racial and social justice within
urban communities so that black neighborhoods can have access to the
resources that would allow them to create their own role models and
have their own youth groups. Without listening, allowing those within
struggling communities to make the calls about how to best raise their
children, and empowering these same communities with much needed
and deserved resources, all white folks are doing is subconsciously
recreating a reality for these kids that white communities are safe and
black communities are unsafe. Without critically reflecting on our
educational materials, sexual violence educators may be teaching those
same racist lessons.

And one more thing: if you are a middle-class white church that
buses in black kids from poor urban areas, don't pass around a collection
plate at the end of youth group and ask for an financial offering that
would bless the speakers that evening. Seriously, this happened and I
almost threw up.

# Redemption

Looking back and taking a deep breath, I realize that I should make something clear: not all the churches we stopped at were appalling. In fact, because we actually had more positive experiences at churches than negative ones, we made it a point to use them as our first resource on Sundays and Wednesdays. On Sundays we would try to stop by a church in the morning looking to catch a service in the hopes that we would either get to say a few words about our cause or at least get a shout out from the pastor at the pulpit. On Wednesday nights we would try and coincide our evening break with a Bible study. Our strategies often provided resources when we needed a place to stay and we were almost always fortunate to find loving people inside that welcomed us in and fed us great food. In these regards, churches were usually a win-win situation. They had plenty of people who were willing to help and they had plenty of people who were willing to listen to what we had to say. It wasn't often that we found a better forum with an audience already in place and anxious to hear from us.

The first great experience I remember having at a church was about week after we got stuck out in the rain in Southern Florida. As usual, it was late and we needed a place to stay. By now this seemed like a common theme, but then again, walking everyday for three straight months offers up that type of monotony. We knocked on the door looking for a way in when a car pulled around front and a man rolled down the window and asked if he could help us. We said were wondering if we could stay at the church and without hesitation he said, "Well, no one's here right now, but you can stay at my place."

Oblivious to what he just said, Kate continued the conversation in her plea-like manner trying desperately to explain to the man that we were poor, lost, wondering souls who were trying to make a difference yet ever so tired and weary. Rebecca and I just looked on in bewilderment allowing Kate to continue her speech in total disregard. It was amusing and I was looking for entertainment. When she finally finished, the man just shook his head and avoided eye contact. As he began to open his door, I approached the car an introduced myself as if apologizing for Kate's oblivion that he had already offered a place.

"Hi sir, I'm Josh."

"Hi, I'm Stan," he replied. "If you all don't mind, you're more than welcome to come home with me."

We moved around to the back of the car as he opened his trunk and shuffled a few things around. From the looks of the contents within the trunk, he was some sort of handy-man. There were hammers and drills and saws and wire-cutters. All the gaps between the larger tools were scattered with displaced screws and bolts, nails and washers. Rebecca and I helped Kate along like a misguided freshman on a big new campus looking for the library. Still in confusion over what just happened, we stripped her of her bag, threw it in the trunk, and hurried her into the back seat.

With Rebecca up front, Kate leaned over to me in the back seat and whispered, "What just happened?" I explained Stan's position on the whole matter and Kate slowly settled back into her seat with her back erect and eyes staring forward against the driver's headrest. It looked as if she was still processing the entire ordeal. We were all fatigued.

Stan, who we had affectionately and uncreatively began referring to as "Stan the Man," is quite possibly the most hospitable person I have ever met. On the ride back to his home he told us the abbreviated story of his life and how he was the volunteer maintenance person at the church. And if I recall correctly, Stan the Man's whole life currently consisted entirely of volunteer work. If I had to guess, Stan the Man was in his late-sixties and from the sound of it, he had some financial success before he retired and was now living out the rest of his days purely on savings. But because he didn't like the sound of "retirement," he volunteered doing handy-man work at local churches and shelters.

When we pulled into his driveway at the end of a long gravel country road, we were greeted by the other occupants of his small, three room ranch-house. Stan the Man must have had seven or eight cats roaming around his property. He said they were all stays that had wandered over after he started feeding and caring for one, but that he only took care of their basic needs. None of them ever went into the house.

Getting inside the air-conditioning was a luxury. The cool hardwood floors wrapped around my throbbing feet. Once we were inside, Stan didn't say much beyond, "This is your home for the night. Do whatever you'd like."

Immediately, Kate asked the one questioned we were always wanting an answer for, "Can we take a shower?"

"This is your home," Stan calmly replied. "No more questions."

With that, I plopped on his couch and began riffling through the channels. I was anxious to catch up on the news about the recent fires that had started up in Florida. So far we had managed to maneuver around them, but they were hot on our trail (pun intended) and looking to burn us (pun intended, again). Looking back, I don't know how we avoided all those fires that broke out throughout Florida during the summer of 2008, but if I was a betting man, I would bet that something bigger than us was looking out for our best interest and the interest of the cause. It's the only logical explanation seeing that areas we had passed through were only one or two days away from going up in flames and several highways that we had recently walked along were now closed down for several days at a time due to the fires.

After only about 15 minutes at Stan's, he said he had to leave.

"What?" I asked.

"Yeah, I have a meeting at church later tonight with the elders," he said and then followed up with, "You all do whatever you'd like and I'll be home in about two hours. The only thing you can't do is eat the homemade apple pie on the stove. It's for the Bible study tomorrow night. They made a special request for my homemade apple pie." Then with a hint of pride he added, "It's *really* good. I make it from scratch."

Before he mentioned the pie, I hadn't even noticed it. But once he mentioned the pie, it was as if its aroma was intentionally assaulting my nostrils. It was taunting me and asking me to give in to my temptation. But I wouldn't. I couldn't! Stan had just given us complete access to his entire home and was entrusting us with everything he owned. The least I could do was respect the delicious pie that stared me down from within the kitchen.

As he predicted, Stan the Man returned home in about two hours. He brought with him a pepperoni pizza and an element of good news.

"Hey everyone!" He boasted as he walked through the front door in a voice that was more energetic and contradictory to his composed demeanor earlier. "I went ahead and picked up a pizza. Hope you're hungry."

We huddled around the island in the kitchen and dug into the hot pizza. Pizza had become a food we had all grown to crave. The trip was funny like that. For some reason there were a few foods that we all seemed to want while on the trip that prior to the trip had no appeal to us. It was reminiscent of all those stories I had heard about women who became pregnant and had to satisfy weird taste buds that they never knew they had before. In addition to pizza, we all consumed a lot of soda, which was something I almost never drank back home. Of course drinking soda in such a physically demanding setting seems counterintuitive, but it makes sense that we would want something so rotten for us after a long day of chugging down gallons upon gallons of nutritious and tasteless water.

Something else I craved was that apple pie that Stan had sitting on his oven. With that thought fresh in my mind, Stan dropped a bombshell.

"I went to church tonight and told them that they get me all the time," he paused as if trying to build the suspense, "So I told them I'd make them another pie some other time. That one on the stove is all yours."

Adding to my elevated celebration was the fact that there was vanilla ice-cream sitting in the freezer just waiting for its opportunity to become alamode atop a piping hot slice of delicious apple pie.

# Abandoned Gas Stations and Stray Dogs

**D**uring the planning of this trip there were plenty of critics putting up verbal blocks. Whether their sarcastic tone or cynical attitudes were intentional or unintentional are irrelevant to the effect that those words had on our spirits and the effect they had on our determination. In my assessment, poor attitudes from others only made us want to succeed even more if for no other reason than to shut people up. It seemed as if everywhere we turned we were bombarded with questions of planning and precaution about the dangers of such a task. A particular question thrown out by all the haters was that of where we would stay. Many suggested that we make prior arrangements with local churches and shelters before taking off. After all, we already had a set agenda as to where we would be by the end of each night so it wouldn't be difficult to look up a few places online that happened to be in the area. But we were insistent on letting the chips fall where they may. Besides, what good is an adventure if you plan out every detail ahead of time? Part of the appeal of such a journey was not knowing what new stories would unfold each day.

On the whole, this plan, or rather lack of plan, worked out well. In total, we only camped out four or five nights over the course of three months and those nights were always in someone's backyard. It was nice never having to pitch a tent in a city park or in a field on the side of the road. In hindsight, we were extremely fortunate and blessed to never have to succumb to such circumstances. This trip has really renewed my faith in the generosity and hospitality of other people. However, there were a few times when a little extra planning would have been to our benefit. Particularly when it came to doing a little a research about the size of the towns we would be staying in.

As I've mentioned before, we walked 20 miles a day on average. Some days it was less and some days it was more and most of the time the days where we had to walk more were unintentional and uninvited. The days when we had to walk extra miles happened because we simply had no other choice but to move forward for a lack of resources at certain destinations. For example, one town we had planned to stop at in Northern Florida happened to be an on-ramp for the interstate. There was no food, no shelter, no houses, and no people. There was just a slightly used on-ramp that had a stake in the ground near its base that declared the name of a non-existent town. Fortunately, a mile up the road there were a few signs of civilization and we were able to bed down in a Comfort Inn.

While it was rarely needed because of the generous hospitality we received throughout the trip, we did budget one hotel room per week for showers and relaxing beds or, in this instance, a lack of any safe alternatives.

A day after leaving the Comfort Inn we crossed the border out of Florida and into Georgia. This was quite possibly the happiest I had been so far during the walk. Turning the corner on a winding road I could see the small, dingy blue bridge that lay about a half-mile up ahead in the distance. Although humble in its appearance, for us it was the entrance into the promise land. The bridge's modest appearance appealed to me like something sanctified. I imagine that Indiana Jones probably had a similar thought process when picking out the unassuming chalice that Christ drank from known as the Holy

Grail. Much like the bridge, the cup wasn't covered in gold and jewels, but he knew it was special. Now even though the bridge into Georgia didn't have any life or death implications for myself or Sean Connery, I still think the experiences of Indiana Jones and me are relatable.

Within a few minutes of walking toward the bridge, I had spotted the backside of a "Welcome to Florida" sign. We all paused for a minute and soaked in the moment. Kate removed the camera and began snapping pictures of our elated faces as Rebecca and I stripped our packs and climbed all over the sign – hugging it like a lost dog we had finally found. However, this lost dog had some flees and because it took me 400 miles to find him, I was without remorse when I deserted the dog and ran towards the more appealing mutt.

(Oh yeah! In case you're wondering where you can get a copy of those hilarious pictures, I'm here to tell you that you can't. Kate sort of accidentally deleted all of the pictures somewhere in South Carolina. Rebecca and I actually thought this whole situation was funny, but for some reason Kate never found the humor in it.)

Running towards the bridge to Georgia, I know I had to have looked ri-dic-u-lous. I knew this because what I was doing wasn't really running or any movement really associated with running. In all that gear, my movements were probably more accurately described as an awkward waddle. It was probably similar to the walking style of a duck who had busted knee caps.

During this ungraceful, yet epic, moment, I reached into my fanny pack and removed my iPod. This required theme music and I wasn't about to let my movie scene go stale. Due to the confused emotions stirring within me, it took me a second to figure out how to best express myself through someone else's art (isn't it comical how we stress our individuality by filling our lives with creative things other people have produced?). Anyway, I digress. The song I settled on was *Georgia on My Mind* by Ray Charles. I believe my reasons are self explanatory.

I did think about using the theme from *Rocky*, but we would be in Philadelphia in a month.

For those paying attention, there were two details here I would like to elaborate on. First, yes I wore a fanny pack for the duration of the trip. Kate and Rebecca tried to subdue their urges, but six weeks in they would eventually give in to the fashionable temptation. In actuality, fanny packs just made it easier to store the maps, phones, cash, and a few other things one may need access to without the hassle of taking off a pack – something you rarely want to do because it's so hard to put it back on both physically and emotionally. Second, while I did have an iPod with me throughout the trip, I surprisingly rarely used it. I brought it along to have alternative options to boredom, but seeing that most of the East Coast was populated with a captive audience, I was too busy making conversation to listen to music.

After waddling across the bridge, which we had to do quickly because there were no shoulders and cars were coming, I turned around one last time to view what had been our enemy for three weeks. The entire state of Florida. I hated Florida in that moment and was glad to be out of that stupid, stupid state. In the dense Georgia heat, which was surprisingly similar to the heat we had just left in Florida, I vowed never to enter that dreaded place again.

A few paces into Georgia, I realized what a blessing Florida had been. Don't get me wrong, I wasn't trying to get back together with Florida, but Florida had sidewalks and large shoulders along the road. You know, she did little things like that that made me want to stay in the relationship and now that we were no longer together I realized how much I underappreciated her. From my assessment, Georgia hated sidewalks and the shoulders of the roads were about as wide as a balance beam. This forced us to stumble through the high grass every now again, which wasn't safe and extremely idiotic on our part given all the snakes and alligators in those parts. However, during this time we were less concerned with the animals that could emanate poison or potentially eat us and more concerned with the giant, hamster-size bugs. Seriously, what is the deal with the bugs in Georgia? There were actually a few instances where I swatted at a bug and it punched me in the mouth. I even witnessed a car-jacking incident after a careless driver left his keys in the ignition when he got out of his car to assess the front-bumper damages caused by a dragon-fly!

Aside from the bugs and the Rottweiler that almost ate off our faces because some people in the South don't believe in leash laws or fences, Georgia was great. We trekked through the heat that first day with a renewed energy pulsing through our legs and feet even though the humidity was thick enough to need a machete to cut through its density. Having a machete may have even been useful on that dog (only for protection PETA). But I managed to do without. The first day in Georgia was unique in that it was the first day where we walked for over six miles at a time without seeing anyone or anything. This made us even more cautious in making sure to stop at every available public facility in order to fill up on water and rest in the shade. As we noticed that the time of day was just past four, a sense of anxiety crept into us because we were unsure of where we were. And with no road signs or mile markers, it was impossible to tell just how far we needed to go to get...somewhere. Within a few minutes, we had reached a clearing where there were no longer trees lining each side of the road. Instead of trees, old trailers and dilapidating houses scattered the side of the road. The rusted cars parked on the unpaved driveways made it difficult to tell if these buildings were even inhabited. Toys were thrown about the yards and chain-linked swings swung gently when they would catch a breeze. Finally, we reached a marked road sign.

This couldn't be right. Could it?

We had entered the town Colesburg, Georgia. However, I wonder if I can even use the word "town" so loosely when describing an area so small and seemingly abandoned merely to discover that its only inhabitants were a boarded up gas station and a stray dog. Unlike the face eating Rottweiler we had passed earlier, this dog was unriled by our presence almost to the point where I wondered if it was even alive. The black mutt was dirty and its head slouched as if in shame. It wore a coat so unkempt that I could see the poor dog's roughen texture and the matted hair beginning to lock in place.

I sat down on a concrete block under some shade provided by the abandoned gas station realizing that these bricks could tumble and the awning could cave at any moment. The lack of population and general disconcern this area had for the structural integrity of public buildings led me to believe that should a cave-in happen, no one would have even noticed and we would have never been found. I wondered how many other small towns had been lost and forgotten like Colesburg – their memories trapped inside rotting buildings and beat down dogs never to be released. What had happened here? Who had lived here? And with all this questioning, and perhaps due to the weight of hopelessness that was heavy on my shoulders, I died a little too.

Defeated, we sat and thought for a moment. Looking back, I don't know why we sat and thought. Perhaps "thinking" is just one of those things we do as a formality. Thinking being an act to illustrate that we are not sporadic and irrational, but that we take our time and combed through our options. But really, and we knew this long before we sat down to "think," there was only one option – keep walking. For all rational purposes, we couldn't stop here for the night with no food, water, or shelter and we knew that a similar sized town, at least according to the map, was up the road about three or four miles. But we were cautious not to get our hopes up. The town up ahead may not even have a dog.

Walking under the sun, which was increasingly hotter, my head hung low and I counted my steps. One, two…one hundred. Then again. One, two…one hundred. Again. One, two…one hundred. Over and over and over again. One, two…one hundred. I couldn't tell you how long this went on, but I know how it stopped. It stopped when a car that had flown ahead of us just moments ago had turned around and skidded to a stop in the gravel parking lot of some run down country store.

"Hey, I've seen you all out here a few times today while on my way back and forth between home and town. What are you all up to? It ain't like there's much going on out here."

His name was Jack and he was a local architect and small-town political pundit. By the time he caught up to us, we had walked over 23 miles in the unforgiving heat and were drained in everyway one can imagine. With his window rolled down, he began explaining to us a few of the local particulars of the area: the landscape, the small towns, and the Southern hospitality. He was a warm and inviting man with a trimmed white beard and a hint of laughter in every word that rolled off his tongue. Yet despite all his positive qualities, I admit that during this whole exchange of polite formalities I was more focused on the air-conditioning pouring out of his car than the words pouring out of his mouth.

"There's a town about two miles up. They're having a town hall meeting at 5:30 tonight. If you'd like, I can drive you into town."

With little deliberation, we piled into his car. Given our large packs, uncomfortable seating was always expected any time we got in a car. Still, Jack's car had the added obstacle of blueprints and carpentry tools. We somehow managed to fit and agreed that the air-conditioned box we were crammed into was better than the alternative. Pulling into town, a two minute drive that would have taken us an additional hour, Jack dropped us off in the back of a simple, small-town church. It was our feeling that we may as well begin hunting for places to stay since we had some time before the town hall meeting. The church and the few elders inside looked as if they had been decorated that way for the last hundred years. They were immaculately kept and shimmering. Everything looked freshly painted and the siding and fences were a blinding shade of white. One of the elders told us that Bible study that night did not start until seven, but that we were more than welcome to come back and they would likely be able to help us out with some indoor lodging. God's people had once again redeemed their cursed brethren of Southern Florida.

Hungry, we walked back to the main road that shot through the middle of town. Approaching the road I realized the quaintness of it all. This town was quite literally a one mile stretch down Main Street. With local shops, businesses, and churches on either side, the buildings were in a perfectly straight line that seemed to be untouched by the last 50 years of globalization. I stood at the North end of town able to see the South edge without as much as a squint of my eyes. It was uncanny how perfectly put together this little slice of land was and how foreign it was to me to be in a place untouched by Wal-Marts and Starbucks. Finally, we spotted a gas station a block down.

Grabbing up a few pre-packaged sandwiches and a two-liter of soda, we returned outdoors to the rapidly changing weather. Across the street was a different, and significantly larger, church than the one we had stopped by twenty minutes ago. We ran through what had turned into a torrential downpour toward the canopy shelter the church provided and it was here where we enjoyed our dinner. Listening to the enormous droplets crash against the windows and metal roofing, I unloaded my sleeping mat and sleeping bag for a more comfortable sit on the cool concrete. At 5:15 pm we re-packed our belongings and headed for the town hall. The rain was still coming down hard, but in a town this size nothing was more than a few feet away and made the weather seem irrelevant.

Entering the town hall was fantastic. In a town of twelve hundred people, Woodbine, Georgia certainly has its politics together for those who would care to get involved. The room was arranged to seat fifty and about three-fourths of the seats were filled. We sat in the back unsure of how our presence would be taken. Additionally, the odor from our clothes was now a blend of sweat, sunscreen, and wet dog and made us rather self-conscious. We didn't want to upset anyone. When Jack entered we left our chairs and huddled around him as if to say to the rest of the town's folks, "See, Jack knows us!" Jack was fumbling to carrying a set of blueprints and poster boards, which made introductions awkward.

He hurried to the opposite end of the room and placed his materials on the table to make our announcement more professional.

Cordially, the city council invited us forward to speak and we were informally placed at the top of that night's agenda. It is fairly indicative of a great community when the city council rearranges its agenda in order to extend warm greetings and hospitality to visitors. Making Kate our designated speaker, she once again ran through our agreed upon mission statement, but this time the three of us seemed more inspired than usual and Rebecca and I casually chimed in where appropriate. After all, this so far was our biggest, most attentive audience and it just felt natural to make this into a conversation as opposed to a lecture. At the end of our presentation we each gave a quick bio about ourselves and then fielded a few questions about the trip.

Getting reacquainted with our chairs, we relaxed into the rest of the town's meeting. The major topic of the evening was the restoration of an old theatre. This apparently was what all of Jack's clutter was about. After giving a passionate explanation and laying out the details of a timeline and budget, the members voted to keep pushing Jack's idea forward. I was extremely pleased with Jack's presentation style and excited about the town's new project to restore what they consider a small part of their history. Woodbine was unwilling to allow those stories to be locked away in a vault behind boarded up windows and concreted doorways.

About an hour had passed and the meeting was over. Like good hosts and hostesses, the people in the meeting encircled us afterwards and began asking follow-up questions they had been thinking about throughout its duration. A woman named Libby probably asked the most welcomed questioned of them all.

"Where are ya'll staying tonight?"

Not wanting to seem desperate, Kate shyly responded, "There's a possibility at a church across the street, but we don't really know."

In rapid responses, Libby offered, "Well, my husband Mike and I have a bed and breakfast with extra rooms if you'd like."

Rebecca and I were within eavesdropping distance of Kate and Libby's conversation and upon hearing Libby's offer we both glanced over and gave Kate a nodding approval. Kate immediately accepted.

Like parishioners exiting on a Sunday morning, we stepped outside the town hall into the clearing skies and congregated with the small clusters of folks who were slowly making their journey home. It's not so much that they were moving slowly as it seemed that they were in no rush to leave the presence of their friends at the meeting. A nice woman with ebony skin and deep wrinkles – not wrinkles that make a person look old, but wrinkles that make a person look wise – approached us and asked if we were headed down to the local restaurant to eat with everyone. Rumor had it that several of the local folks involved with town hall meetings regularly gathered afterwards at a local restaurant to break bread and enjoy each other's company. Upon hearing that Mike and Libby were among the regulars, we confirmed that we would in fact be joining them.

We literally walked directly across the street to Mike and Libby's for a quick drop off of our belongings and a quick exchange of clothes. Within minutes we arrived at what we would soon learn was the only restaurant in town. Captain Stan's was a shack of sorts that smelled like aged wood and collard greens. The shack itself was small, but we were informed that most folks ate outside on the picnic tables enclosed by a seven foot tall fence.

Opening the gate I saw the rendition of what looked like a gypsy campground. There was an oddity of sorts that piled up out here and it was accompanied by the smell of stale beer and fried food that soaked into the nooks and crannies. In a back corner, the corner that connected with the shack, there was a tiki-bar and in the opposite corner was a performance stage so rugged and worn I could almost hear the timeless songs and stories of local legends deeply embedded in the floorboards.

Most of the picnic tables in the stage area had been set up end to end, which was indicative of the family connection many of these people felt towards one another. We moved two large picnic tables together under the cooling night and began soaking up the friendly atmosphere.

Embracing my surroundings, I ordered everything Southern and washed it all down with the most delicious sweet tea that has ever passed over my lips. After listening to the entertaining stories of small town living and debating both local and national politics, we carved our names into the wooden fence right next to all the other local celebrities and left for home. Or rather, we left for the fluid space that had become home for us. With our laundry secured in that lovely device know as the washing machine, we crawled into our king-sized beds and sank beneath the soft white sheets. I don't even remember my head hitting the pillow.

We woke up the next day and were unexpectedly greeted by an enticing proposition. I believe it was a Thursday, but either way, it was finals week at the local high school and Mike was a teacher. Libby had made us a filling breakfast complete with eggs, biscuits, and gravy. As I ate my meal and sipped lemonade on the screened-in porch, Libby entered and offered a gift.

"I don't want to be too pushy and I know ya'll gots a schedule, but if you'd like you could stay here for the day and relax for a while."

This was the first time during the trip that the opportunity of taking the day off had even been a possibility.

"Don't rush," Libby continued noticing the panicked deliberation in my eyes, "I have to run to the store. You finish breakfast and wake the girls. Ya'll can talk it over and let me know when I get back."

After gathering seconds and putting them down faster than the firsts, I ever so quietly approached the room where Kate and Rebecca were sleeping. Slowly opening the door, my bare feet creaked across the hardwood floor, and the texture of that old wood on my feet caused an euphoric rush through my legs and up into chest. The bedding was so fluffed and piled high that I couldn't even see their heads, but just two lumps in the sheets rising and falling ever so gently, which was indicating that something alive and breathing must be under there. My voice broke the quiet sounds of morning and Kate and Rebecca stirred awake. I informed them about Libby's proposition and without hesitation they both eagerly agreed and returned back to sleep, enjoying that bed for a good 20 more minutes.

When Libby finally arrived back home, Kate and Rebecca were in the kitchen eating breakfast. I was back on the porch reading *The Autobiography of Malcolm X. The Autobiography of Malcolm X* was the one book I kept with me on the walk. Through Florida, I was too busy getting over the initial shock of actually walking up the East Coast and too tired at the end of every day to even think about cracking open a book. Now that we were going to get a 24-hour break from walking, I figured I could begin to indulge in a little mental stimulation. You know, learn about someone else's quest for social change and how they got their start.

We relaxed until eleven o'clock or so before Libby finally informed us of the master plan she had been scheming since last night.

"About 20 miles from here, there's a big resort that I can get us into. It's like a country club for politicians. There's a golf course, cabins, and hunting. If you'd like, we can go out there and ride golf carts around the property. It's really beautiful and right on the water."

The plan sounded fine by us, especially Rebecca. Anytime she could get near the water was a good time in her life. Getting there was a beautiful trip in and of it self. Traveling the back roads gave me ample time to enjoy the sights and sounds of nature without feeling it in my feet or back. The lodge was right across the channel that looked over to Cumberland Island, and the landscape was even more pristine then Libby had explained. After getting in touch with one of Libby's old friends who still worked the grounds, we got a guided tour of the place.

I drove Libby around in one of the golf carts and she told me the history of the place and her place in it. Apparently, this club was frequented by a lot of Republican politicians. She then added that the club frequented by Democratic politicians was about 30 minutes up the road.

As Libby spoke of that old place, I could see her getting younger. Years shed off her face as she pointed out landmarks made infamous by her youth. She would hear birds calling out to one another and recall the long past teachers who had taught her how to identify each song. The three hour tour ended at a small cabin over looking the water. The cabin was a glorified snack bar with a connected swimming pool and hot tub. Inside was a jukebox and I quickly put that thing to use by punching in G-0-0-1-0. With Kate and Rebecca at the bar enjoying soda and pretzels, I grabbed Libby by the hand and we tore up the door floor allowing the Temptations' *The Way You Do the Things You Do* to carry the movement of our bodies.

All of us went home that night feeling a whole lot better both physically and mentally. The day off was exactly what we needed right then. Mike and Libby had invited some friends over that night for dinner and once again the smell of Southern cooking filled the air. I set the table on the screened-in porch watching the day disappear behind the far off trees. When we had all sat down and finished saying grace, we began to take our fill of smoked salmon, asparagus, corn bread, mashed potatoes, and garlic bread. And staying true to the South, I rinsed it down with mouth-watering sweet tea.

The next morning on our way out, Jack stopped by to drop off a few presents. Given the constant sun exposure we were receiving he felt it necessary to provide us with hats, which we graciously accepted and wore nearly everyday for the remainder of the trip. After snapping a few pictures and signing Libby and Mike's guest book, we left Woodbine much like we had left every other place we had stayed, quietly and peacefully – disappearing down the road and fading into the backdrop of the horizon among the blacktop and the tress.

# Redemption II

For the rest of our time in Georgia we were constantly walking in and out of small towns unsure of which ones would be able to help us out and which ones had been abandoned like Colesburg. There was even one time when we were walking through a desolate stretch between towns and we got stuck in the pouring rain for ten miles with no shelter. This wasn't all bad seeing that the rain did keep the bugs away and cooled the air. Yet it did cause quite a few of our possessions to get soaked. Because of situations like this, anxiety was constant. We wanted to make sure that we walked at least 20 miles everyday so that we wouldn't get behind schedule, but we also didn't want to pass up an accommodating town in the late afternoon if it offered us a safe and dry place to stay that night. We knew that without knowing what was ahead, there was always a chance of us ending up in the middle of nowhere once the sun finally set.

Fortunately for us, Highway 17 was slowly making its way back toward the coast, which usually indicated more people and more resources. A few days after leaving Woodbine, we found ourselves in a confusing location where interstates and highways were meeting up and splitting apart and it was our job to figure our which way was North all while avoiding the cars either getting on or getting off the highway. After being turned around a couple of times we finally made it out of the highway mess and were heading North on our beloved 17. Though by the time we finally got things sorted out it had become late in the day and so we decided it best to try and find some place to stay. About three miles up the road from all the chaotic traffic sat a little church back on a hill. Quite poetic sounding, I know. There weren't any cars in the parking lot, but the sign out front was inviting everyone in for Bible study that night so we marched up the hill and plopped ourselves down right on the front porch. Too exhausted to even get a drink, the three of us began to drift in and out of sleep and before long we had all fallen into a deep nap.

Dirty and sleeping, we must have looked pathetic when the pastor finally discovered us about an hour later. All I remember was the sound of a car pulling over some gravel and then a large figure was standing above me.

"Well, what do we have here?" He said in a rather fascinating and playful tone.

Stumbling to my feet and trying to compose myself the best I could for a someone who had just woken up wearing the same dirty clothes that hadn't been washed for a few days, I searched my mind for the script I had recited so many times before.

"Hello sir," I began, "The three of us have been walking since Miami to raise awareness about sexual violence."

"You don't say."

"Um yes, I do say," I said clumsily still not picking up on his sarcasm. "Anyway, we saw your sign out front about the Bible study tonight and we were hoping that your congregation might be able to help us out."

His eyes grew big and he began to chuckle. I stared at him waiting for a verbal response, but he said little as he opened the front door and motioned for us to enter the lobby.

"You know, God's funny like that," he said reflexively.

"What do you mean?"

"What I mean is that our church just entered into this whole new mission about a month ago. It's a series about meeting people needs. Meeting people where they're at."

He continued, "If you all need a place to stay, then that's how we can best serve you."

A rush passed over me and a renewed sense of faith entered my spirit. There was no skepticism and no sarcasm. There was just some good ol' fashion love thy neighbor. The pastor showed us around the building and explained all the new additions they had just made to the church. To our good fortune, they had just installed new bathrooms with showers late last fall after they received funding to take care of homeless folks during the winter. Apparently, for a few of the coldest weeks in the winter, congregation members would take turns sleeping over at the church so that it could stay open to folks who needed a warm place to rest overnight. The cots for this operation had been placed in storage for the summer, which meant we didn't have beds, but we did have plenty of room on the mats in the children's classrooms.

By the time we took a quick shower and got dressed, it was already time to head over to the fellowship hall for Bible study. The pastor must have told the members about his guests because as we entered people began to get out of their seats in order to come greet us. Like the town hall meeting in Woodbine, the pastor invited us up front to give a presentation about our mission and we did our best to respond to the each parishioner's questions. During this time, the pastor just stood behind us rocking back and forth with a grin that stretched from ear to ear.

When we returned to our seats, the pastor went into an impromptu sermon about the Good Samaritan and how it was the church's job to take in beaten down kids from the streets when they were strewn out across your doorsteps. Even though his words were rough and the way he described us was rather jarring, he spoke in a good-natured tone so I didn't let it bother me any. Besides, these folks were giving us a clean room for the night so the least I could do was to let them have a laugh or two at our expense. These church folks had good hearts and saw our situation as an opportunity from God for them to serve. We were just happy to be on the receiving end of that blessing.

Along with our personal blessings, what was equally as exciting about this particular church on this particular night was that the Bible study was showcasing a short documentary about another small Southern church that was also trying to meet the everyday needs of everyday people, but was doing so in a much more elaborate way. I'll admit that at first I was a little sketchy about what this movie was all about. Based on previous church experiences, I had pictured some street corner preacher telling everyone that all their problems would be solved if they just believed in Jesus. But thankfully, I was wrong.

In reality, the church shown in this documentary did very little preaching with its mouth at all. Interviews with some of it members illustrated that they were far more concerned with preaching with their actions. They worked on the hope that people would feel invited into their church by seeing a loving community as opposed to hearing fundamentalist yelling about hell fire and brimstone. Two of the more "controversial" subjects they dealt with were teen pregnancy and abortion. To the best of my knowledge, mainstream Christianity has an opinion on both matters and in both instances the answers are "no" and "no." So you can imagine my surprise when I discovered that there was actually a church out there who had support groups for teenage girls who had become pregnant and teenage girls who had had abortions.

Although this church didn't support abortion, they were taking all the steps necessary to make sure that the mother-to-be had access to the resources once the baby was born. For me, this is a position I can support. I mean, it makes sense that if a church wants to be anti-abortion, then they had better be willing to take in unwed mothers who need help and adopt newborn babies that would have otherwise been aborted. Too often nowadays, it just seems as if the Church only cares about babies getting born. After that, many churches seem to be indifferent about the quality of life that children and young mothers have.

To sum up the rest of the movie and the position of that small town church in Georgia that I believe we can all learn from, I would say that they were simply proactive instead of reactive. It's popular, and easier, to jump on board a religious debate after the flames have been ignited without attending to the lives of everyday people, but this church had consciously chosen to remove itself from the debate over dogma and decided to do the best they could for their community. They seemed to understand that theories don't conquer injustice and if things were going to change for the better, than they needed to take risks and explore supportive methods that may elicit change. Every day they were showing their community that they were concerned about other people's needs and they were tirelessly making an effort to meet people on a practical level. For example, instead of telling parents to be more loving toward each other, they set up free baby-sitting services so that parents could have a date night. Instead of telling people to pray for prosperity, they were setting up job training workshops and relational tithes where people could get help with their bills until they found a job. Instead of telling people to get off drugs, they had Alcoholic and Narcotic Anonymous meetings for people to access support without feeling judged about stepping foot into a church while they were addicted. From my perspective, this church had it together because they were making the effort to become more inclusive of the outside community. They were being compassionately active instead of passive with their message of hope, faith, and love.

Like any programs set up within the confines of an organization, I imagine this church is not without its faults and I'm certain that it makes mistakes. But then again, the only people who don't make mistakes are the people who sit around and do nothing. The people who don't make mistakes are the ones who dream up theories for fixing problems, but they never take any practical steps that might actually lead to finding solutions for those problems. To be clear, the three of us made many mistakes on this walk. I'm sure there are far better ways to go about educating the general public about sexual violence than walking the East Coast, and we recognize that our methods may have been imperfect. But despite the imperfections, what's important is that both the church's programs and we as walkers were trying out ideas aimed at helping others.

I like to think that innovative approaches try to break free from (or at least, put to good use) the bondage of theoretical frameworks and elitist discourses about change and attempt to put those ideas into action. Sure there were plenty of projects at this church that needed to be deconstructed when it came to being more conscious about issues of class, race, gender, and sexual orientation. Likewise, I know that the same was true of our walk. However, I refuse to critically tear into an organization that is doing the best they can with the resources they have without offering up different possibilities. Plus, I would say these church folks were working far better than most charities because they were willing to *listen* to their neighbors. They were engaging in progressive conversations about how to move forward with their message of hope, faith and love in a more inclusive way. For example, the poor area of their community was mostly African-American and instead of going in with all the answers like a contemporary great white hope, this church began asking African-American community leaders in the area questions about what their church could do, and if in fact the black community wanted their church to do anything at all! Imagine that, a church with resources asking people in need if what the church has to offer will help them opposed to assuming they know all the answers.

In the end, it was the tenacity of this church that set it apart from other churches I've been in. They were taking risks in areas that several mainstream churches refuse to go. They knew that they were going to make mistakes because there were so few examples to model their programs after. Yet when it came down to it, they were unwilling to give up just because they had gotten it wrong a few different times. They knew they would fail at some of their projects and that other projects would get messy, but instead of trashing the whole vision and retreating to the safety of conversing only gospel, this church embraced the struggle along the lines of class, race, and gender and decided to stick with their progressive message no matter how many times they may fail.

Similarly, it is the progressive effort of trial and error that I like to think our walk against sexual violence was situated. The three of us were imperfect and we carried a difficult message imperfectly into imperfect homes, diners, churches, and communities. However, at the end of the day we were trying something new and creative in the hopes of generating conversations about an issue that we can rest assured will not go away if we choose to be silent just because we have yet to find the perfect solution.

The following morning, the pastor came by before we left and gave us the number of a church 20 miles up the road at our next stop. He had called them the night before and made arrangements for them to be waiting for us that evening. The pastor also gave us a new map with some shortcuts on it that would take us straight through the next town instead of taking the outside loop around it on Highway 17. It goes without saying that it was much appreciated anytime a local had directions that would get us to the same destination while shaving two or three miles off our route.

About halfway to this new church, we came across a Wal-Mart located in a strip-mall that was peppered with a few fast food restaurants and clothing retail stores. It was early in the afternoon and we hadn't stopped yet since we were racing to that church knowing we had shelter for the evening. Against our collective moral struggle, we decided to pick out a few items from Wal-Mart's deli section and enjoy them in the attached McDonald's. Let the record show that it wasn't our wish to patron Wal-Mart, but someone had given us a $200 gift card before we left so Wal-Mart was already getting paid whether or not we ate there. We figured we should just use it up as quickly as possible so that we could wash the guilt from our hands in a timely manner. Nonetheless, we still felt guilty.

Once we had grabbed our sandwiches and fruit, we settled down into a booth at McDonald's and began eating while making commentary on all the people who passed through the automatic doors. Like many others, I do enjoy the American pastime of people watching, but I like to spice things up a bit and create ridiculous life stories about them. The stories are nothing vulgar or humiliating, but just some laughable anecdotes to entertain myself. After about 30 minutes of this, the creativity was running dry so Rebecca and I decided to leave our booth in order to go pick up a few items. Rebecca needed to get her glasses fixed as they had bent and were constantly falling off of her face and I wanted to get some more super-strength sunscreen because our supply of SPF 40 was running low. I picked out an industrial size bottle of Aloe Vera that smelled like orange creamsicle. It's cheaper to buy in bulk, plus that's the only size Wal-Mart sells. Additionally, I figured this fruity scent would blend nicely and complement the 100 percent DEET bug spay smell that had already permanently imbedded itself in my pores, on my clothes, and throughout my pack. I never said anything about this walk being sexy.

After purchasing a few other essential items, Rebecca and I returned to the booth heartbroken that there was still over $180 left of the gift card. Damn you Wal-Mart and your low prices! At this rate, we would need to start visiting Wal-Mart twice a week if we wanted to deplete the remaining balance of the card before heading home.

"What did you all get?" Kate asked when we got back to the booth.

Rebecca responded, "Some sunscreen, some wet-wipes, and a few snacks."

There was an awkward pause and some strange eye-shifting from Kate as if she was making sure the two of us weren't wired before dropping the code word.

"So," she was leaning in and beginning to whisper, "When you all were gone, I made a friend."

Rebecca and I leaned in waiting for the details.

"So," Kate started again slowly, "some guy just came up and sat down in the booth, and then started asking what I was doing. I just told him a quick version because he was kind of creepy and I was hoping you two would get back soon. And when I was done he told me to wait her for five minutes and he would back."

"How long has it been?" I asked.

"About ten minutes." Kate replied as a matter of fact. And then in a frantic whisper, "Oh my gosh! There he is!"

Rebecca and I glanced briefly and saw a six and a half foot tall man walking towards us in long gangly strides. I don't remember a lot about him except that he wore a light blue shirt and there wasn't a lot of meat on his bones. Also, I remember his hands. His hands were large, maybe even classifiable as gigantic, as they gripped the back of my chair when he leaned in over me.

"Are you two with her?" He asked in a mild manner.

"Yeah," My voice was shaky. I coughed as if clearly my throat, "I'm Josh and this is Rebecca."

There was a long, strange pause that I expected Kate to fill seeing that this was her friend and all, but instead we all just sat there until the man finally spoke again.

"Here," he said shaking my hand and depositing a large amount of cash into my palm.

"Are you sure?" I asked dumbfounded.

"Yeah," he muttered as he turned to walk away. His head hung low and his shoulder slumped like all the wind had just been taken out of his sails. He looked as if an enormous weight had just been taken off his shoulders.

"Wait!" I yelled, "What's your name?"

He stopped and turned slightly so I knew he had heard me, but instead of giving an answer he just gave a slight wave and continued onward. The three of us looked at each other in confusion until Kate finally broke the silence and asked, "How much did he give you?"

"I don't know."

I carefully unfolded the bills under the table and saw that they were all fresh twenties. This man must have left Kate earlier to go make a withdrawal from an ATM.

"Three hundred dollars," I said.

Not knowing what to do, we all continued to stare motionless at one another. A thousand thoughts raced through my mind.

We couldn't accept this! Could we? I mean, people had been giving us a little cash here and there throughout the trip, but that was mostly to cover a meal, not a week's expenses. Well, there was a man who stuffed a $100 bill in my pocket at church last night, but that was at church, not a Wal-Mart. Three hundred dollars was too much!

When someone did finally speak again, it was Kate and she was quick and deliberate.

"Well, I suppose we should get moving."

I left Wal-Mart that afternoon with a mass of mixed emotions. Part of me felt bad for accepting so much money. Part of me wanted to go find that man and give it back. But then another part of me wanted to honor his gift. After all, I did ask him if he was sure about this gift and he was a grown man who purposefully withdrew a large amount of cash from an ATM for the precise reason of passing it on to us. If it was impulsive, he had plenty of time between Kate and the machine and then back to us to change his mind. So in the end, I just stuck the wad of cash into the zip-lock bag that held my other valuables in my fanny pack and I left it alone.

For me, the best visual I could come up with to satisfy my curiosity about his gift was that we were painting a picture and people were beginning to see it. We never went out with the intention of fundraising.

We had done all of that before we left. But as people began to realize that all of our extra cash was going to a women's shelter, they were willing to help. In fact, over the course of the first month of the trip, people had given us so much help on the road financially that we had actually saved money and didn't need to use our debit card for the entire second month. All of our funds sitting in the bank would continue to sit there until we got home and then the extra money would get to go directly to those who needed it: the women and children directly affected by the issue of sexual violence.

We made it to the church that night and I was still wrestling with the situation that had unfolded at Wal-Mart. I don't know why that man had decided to give us such a large amount of money, but I do know that I was thankful. A part of me thinks that either he was hurt or that he watched someone else get hurt and wanted to do something, anything about it. For us, getting to walk the East Coast was a privilege and that was our way of doing something, but we also realize that not everyone has that type of time, ability, and luxury. My suggestion to those who want to do something but don't feel like they can do anything is to be like the man we met in Wal-Mart. Your efforts don't need to be gigantic. Instead, all you have to do is whatever you can do where you're at. For him that meant driving to an ATM and returning with $300 without sharing who he was or why he did it. For others, it might mean donating clothes to a local women's shelter, passing out pamphlets, or most importantly, just being there and believing survivors. We can't always be on the front lines of the fight against sexual violence, but I do believe that we can always find alternative ways to support those who are doing the work everyday.

# Here's to Chad Parker

**A** question that people always ask us has to do with whether or not we walked every step from Miami to Boston. This question bothers me, but not because it makes reservations about our integrity. The question of whether or not we walked the entire stretch of coast bothers me because it seems to be one of the first and most cynical questions people ask. It bothers me because before people have any questions about the stories and struggles of folks we met along the

way, people first want to poke holes in our methods and look for faults in our approach. They want to invalidate us.

Because this particular question became such a staple, I often just address this issue near the beginning of any conversation or presentation about the walk so that people's minds can be at ease and focused. Hence, I wouldn't want our

seemingly suspicious integrity to burn a hole through their conscious and keep them from fully paying attention to the items that really matter. Mainly, how we can all more effectively generate awareness about sexual violence?

With that, the answer is no. No, we did not walk every step between Miami and Boston. Although we thought walking every step would be possible when we first began planning and we even made careful logistical arrangements so that we could indeed perform at such levels, not having the capability of walking every step was simply an unforeseen obstacle that was out of our control.

However, after careful consideration, back-logging, and map checking, I can say the following with complete confidence. In my best estimation, we walked approximately 85% of the entire distance, which translates roughly to about 1,500 miles. Now if people still want to continue being critical about our efforts based on the fact that we did not walk every step, then I have two points I would like to bring to their attention. First, they didn't do it and until they do they are in no position to criticize other people's efforts. To them, I only ask that they walk 1,800 miles over a period of three months. After that, we'll talk. Second, we may not have completed the objective as originally planned, but at least we made one hell of an effort. And truthfully, I think *anyone* who is at least making an effort – any effort – to creatively and passionately bring attention to the issue of sexual violence should be applauded despite the progress being made on a cultural level with tangible outcomes. Those people who are actively advocating against sexual violence are simply ahead of the culture.

Anyway, it was a couple of weeks into the walk when I realized we wouldn't be able to walk every step between Miami and Boston. This realization was both a mental and emotional drain that cut deep. For so long, we had planned this feat only to come to a place where I felt we would somehow be cheating if we accepted a ride down the road. But finally I had to let that disappointment pass and slip into the place where cheating couldn't exist if we were making the rules.

Besides, this was our attempt at activism and our standards would be the ones that measured our feelings of success and accomplishment. I refuse to let our activism be judged by the standards of some critics whose only discussions surrounding activism are negative commentary on someone else's flawed efforts to create change. I knew we wouldn't be able to finish if we were constantly at the mercy of other people's opinions (specifically this guy named Phil who we met at a Taco Bell and who insisted on talking to us even though we wanted nothing to do with his negative remarks). Why was I even allowing other people like Phil to place such a heavy burden on us? Those "other people" weren't out here in the hot sun all day endlessly tracking and trying to bring awareness to an issue that penetrates deep into our social fabric. We soon stopped worrying about the opinions that didn't matter, and we quickly set up our own standards of what was acceptable. What we came up with were three priorities.

First was safety. Safety is a word that encompasses so many things that it's difficult to know or plan for all of the possible hypothetical. A few situations that come to mind were if we were going to enter an area that didn't have necessary resources, we had depleted our resources, or we were in dire need of help, we would be willing to take a ride. For example, we took a couple of short mileage rides through state parks in the middle of the day because local folks had warned us that there were no places available for water for eight to ten miles. Another safety concern was that if the conditions of the route we chose were unwalkable, we would have to look for alternative means of passing through (like riding the ferry across the river). I'll discuss more on unwalkability shortly.

Our second priority was spreading awareness about sexual violence. This may seem like a obvious priority given the fact that this was the only absolute reason for the walk in the first place; however, it became very important for us to redefine and to rethink this objective after we had been on the road for a couple of weeks. As I previously mentioned, people who looked like us (big backpacks and bright teal shirts) got stopped frequently and asked many questions about their purpose. Subsequentially, this made for extremely long days with more stops than we would have preferred. Because of this, we had to give ourselves permission to stop and talk to folks despite our schedule. If we got behind, we knew it was because we were having positive and progressive conversations with folks about the issue we were concerned about. And besides, it seemed counterintuitive to our goals to cut those conversations short just to get on up the road. So in the event that someone invited us to speak at the church or a local media outlet wanted to capture our story, we would willingly take a break for a couple of hours and then have the folks drive us up the road a few miles to counteract the lost time.

Finally, our last priority was that we were determined to walk every step we could between Miami and Boston. Sometimes this required us to get up earlier or be on the road way after dark, but unless the first two priorities trumped our circumstances, we were going to walk regardless of whatever obstacle was thrown before us. And there were quite a few (just keep reading and you'll see why one of my favorite nights was when we were crossing the New York/Connecticut border).

As promised, I wish to revisit the issue of safety since it clearly pertains to the idea of unwalkable areas. While planning, it never occurred to me that unwalkable places would exist along the coast. Call it naiveté, or just plain ignorance, but I imagined all of our route on the East Coast to be only a few feet from water, which meant plenty of coastal property, which also meant plenty of flashy, yet tacky, tourist shops all tricked out with neon signs and full of seashell souvenirs. As facts would have it, I was wrong and I was wrong in the worst way.

Even though I was wrong, I don't much blame myself. Well, at least not entirely. To me, traveling the roads had always been done by car and it seemed reasonable enough that routes that were opened to cars would be easily managed by those who were on foot. Come to find out, I was very much misinformed. In fact, foot travel is quite difficult on main roads that stretch between cities. Even within city limits traveling by foot can be rather dangerous save for the occasional sidewalk; except for Florida where a sidewalk stretches nearly the entire coast. In hindsight, the continuous sidewalks in Florida may have actually been one of the only savory qualities I found in the entire state. Florida, if you are reading this, it's not that I hold anything against you personally, but you must realize the amount of intimidating stress you put on us in those first few weeks of walking.

When areas were absent of sidewalks, we were forced to travel the shoulder. Traveling the shoulder into oncoming traffic wasn't terrible or frightening per se. After all, some shoulders were large and we did see the cars coming at us. This gave us some control over the situation as to how close a proximity we wished to be in relation to an eighteen-wheeler. But then again, some shoulders were small and forced us into the high swampy grasses of Georgia that were rumored to be filled with poisonous snakes and man-eating alligators. Fortunately for Kate and Rebecca, they are women and by definition were unappealing to alligators of the man-eating variety. Fortunately for me, we never came across any alligators and I never got eaten.

We did however come across a few areas where the shoulders were none existent and we were trapped. One area was on a bridge that had one lane closed off due to construction and there were no pedestrian throughways. For a bridge to cross over nearly a mile of water and have no pedestrian accommodations seems rather unacceptable and complete discriminatory to people who don't own cars. In fact, this walk taught me a lot about the car culture in America and how roads are a conspiracy to get people off their legs and addicted to oil. If you don't believe me, take a weekend off and try traveling 50 or 60 miles down the road to some nearby town. Without a car, it's more difficult than you think.

Being unintelligent, we tried crossing the bridge anyway for about 100 yards into on-coming traffic. Having only a few feet between my body and the passing cars I was constantly praying for my life. What made it worse was that the arch of the bridge made it impossible to see the other side so I had no idea how long this was going to go on for. Luckily, I think, we got picked up by the cops. I don't say luckily because they were willing to help us, in fact it was just the opposite. When the cop car stopped in the middle of the road, a very old and very angry man exited. Without much explanation he opened his door, threw our packs in the trunk, and forced all of us into the back seat and onto the cold hard plastic bench. I tried to sit up front so I could play with the sirens, but he denied my request. At that moment, I really thought we were going to be placed under arrest.

The cop didn't say a word to us until he got the end of the bridge, off the main road, and pulled off into a side street. What he said was stern and brief.

"You can't walk across this bridge."

He didn't turn around and stared ahead coldly refusing us even a glance in his review mirror. I grasp the chicken wire and leaned up next to his ear.

"Well, can you just drive us across?"

"No."

"Well, where can we cross?"

"There's a detour bridge about ten miles east."

"We can't walk ten miles there and ten miles back just for a detour! Is there any other way?"

He thought for a moment and then said, "Well, if you want to hitchhike across the bridge, I suppose that would be okay."

We waited for him to let us out of the handle-less back seat doors, which caused me to think, "what if we would have been in an accident and there was a fire and we were trapped in the backseat?" He unloaded our packs as uncaring as he had loaded them, got in his car, and left without a word. Taking a deep breath that was partly a sigh of relief and partly a way to calm our anger, we walked over to McDonald's and began asking strangers for a ride. It only took about 30 minutes of asking before an older, more understanding man with a pickup truck told us that he was heading in that direction. Kate and I hopped in the bed of his pickup, Rebecca in the front, and within a few short minutes we were dropped off in the gravel laced parking lot of a local diner.

A few weeks before this incident at the bridge, we had run into a similarly troubled area along the back roads of South Carolina. We had just crossed over the Georgia/South Carolina state line a few days back and were well refreshed after spending an extra day in the fine town of Savannah with our fabulous hosts Jenny and Danny and their enormous Japanese hunting dog Blue. We came across many fine towns during the walk, but Savannah was particularly fine. The people talk with a slow drawl there and let you know that it's okay to take life a little slower. Being in the South, Savannah's also one of those towns that has the perfect blend of nostalgia that constantly makes me crave collard greens and provides ample opportunity for seeing women in big hoop-skirts and men with funny mustaches.

On this specific day North of Savannah, we had walked about half the distance we were scheduled to walk when we came across a bit of a snag. Much like the bridge, this too was a case of road construction; except here, both shoulders of the road were lined with big orange construction barrels and if we would have attempted to walk it, the distance between the cars and my face would have been non-existent. Making matters worse was the realization that walking in the ditch was nearly impossible and entirely unsafe due to the steep embankment and swampy conditions. I for one didn't care for muddy shoes or the possibility of being snacked on by large reptilian creatures. We were quite literally stuck at the end our rope with no place to go. But, as luck would have it, across the street from the beginnings of this construction dilemma was a homemade pie bakery where we could talk it over. All dire situations just work out better when you solve them over pie.

We dumped our packs on the porch of the small establishment and entered its quaint and homey showroom. The inside felt like the inner workings of a log cabin and had the pleasing aroma of homemade fruit pies. We searched for a few treats and I bought a few extra postcards since I was running low. I had made a habit of trying to send one postcard everyday, or at least every other day, to my partner who was finishing up her dissertation in Colorado. I can't say she was thrilled with me taking off for three months to go hike the East Coast, but she understood and supported the cause.

After grabbing some pie and talking to a few other customers in the shop about how we were trying to raise awareness about sexual violence, we reconvened outside at a picnic table in the small yard of the establishment. We pleasantly discussed our stranded situation with everyone who stopped in for some homemade pie, but everyone was headed in the other direction. At least that's what they said. Seriously, who lies about traveling in the opposite direction when I can clearly see your car leaving ten feet in front of me and heading into the construction? Frustrated, we finally decided to expand our pool of potential helpers from customers in the shop to every passing car heading North. We walked to the edge of the construction zone and then marched across the street so that we were now moving with traffic instead of against it. Against our better judgment and everything taught by horror movies, we stuck out our thumbs and waited in a desolate ditch along a forsaken highway.

During this experiment, my hopes were low and so were our odds. If this had been the on-ramp of an interstate near a populated area, we may have found luck sooner. However, this was a back road in the middle of Podunk, U.S.A. and alternative driving routes were easily accessible. We patiently waited.

For over an hour we took turns standing and sitting. We were sticking our thumbs out as our only means of communication as if our thumbs were switch boards to the nearest taxi service. Finally, after God knows how long, a car pulled into a drive just in front of us and a man in a business suit and slicked back hair rolled down his window.

"Where you all headed?"

"We just need to get up the road past this construction."

Without much further conversation, the man agreed and we climbed in. Once in the car the man was rather talkative, but failed to say much of anything. We did manage to discover that he sold insurance from town to town making a lot of house calls to people who were unable to get to any of the offices for whatever corporation he worked for. Other than that, he just rambled a lot about different customers and started random stories about his life without ever finishing them. In an attempt to move beyond the stale stories of insurance sales, I offered my name and a little information about what we were doing and, at his request, got into some of the more legal issues surrounding sexual violence. His way of communicating was very logically based and he was more interested in the laws of sexual violence opposed to the emotional toll it can have on a person.

When I was done I politely turned the conversation back towards him anticipating a reciprocated response.

"So, what's your name?" I asked.

"Oh, excuse me?" He seemed confused about the depth of such a commonly asked questioned.

"You're name?" I asked once more. This time I was sure to annunciate and allowed each syllable to fully vacate the opening of my mouth before continuing on to the next.

"Um," he staled.

Was he really staling about a question as common and seemingly unobtrusive as to one's name? Even people who are in a witness protection program can answer this question swiftly even if the information they give is falsified and inaccurate. Frankly, he could have said or used any name he wanted. I suppose I wasn't as concerned with the label he was given at birth as I was concerned with the friendliness available when you can refer to a person by their name as opposed to simply, "Hey you." In hindsight, whether or not I had his name was irrelevant to me liking him, I just thought of it as being polite.

His posture changed demeanors and his overt discomfort became covered-up discomfort. With a kind of forced chuckle he said, "Oh, my name isn't important." Then oddly, he quickly and without objective adjusted a few dials on the car's stereo system as if he had a condition that would not allow him to speak and turn dials at the same time. In an effort to cut through the air of awkwardness that hung dense in the car, I sat back and started talking to Kate.

To my surprise, Kate wasn't very talkative. In fact, in all my bidding for this man's name, I had failed to notice that Kate was clinging onto the window and pressing her body deeper and deeper into the back corner of the rear passenger seat.

I leaned in and whispered, "Kate, are you okay?"

"Yeah, I'm just tired"

As I began to sit up and reshape my rear end to the scooped out impression of the bucket seat, Kate viciously attacked my arm. Without a word from either of us, my ear was pulled closely to her lips.

"I don't feel that good and think I'm going to throw up."

I sprang up in a panicked. Quickly, I removed the hat that Jack had given me in Woodbine, Georgia and thrust it into Kate's lap.

"Whatever you do, don't throw up in his car!"

Kate continued, "I think I'm car sick. I haven't been in a car this long for weeks."

It was then when I noticed how perfectly pristine the inside of his car was. He had a shiny dashboard and automatic everything. The leather upholstery was a milky tan color and the carpeted floors looked as if they had just been vacuumed this morning. It wouldn't have surprised me if this car had in fact just been purchased this morning.

Suddenly his phone rang and my attention shifted off of Kate's stomach problems.

"Hello, this is Chad Parker."

What? A name? Yes! I finally found you out Chad Parker! The name "Chad Parker" swirled around in my head like an erotic image of Eden's untouchable fruit. It was like the sacred name that was not to be uttered by the fallible lips of mere mortals. This must have been how Rudy felt when he finally found the buried pirate treasure of One Eyed Willy! The man so secretive of his name had let his guard down and slipped up. Chad Parker had carelessly forgotten that the three of us were sitting next to him in his car and that even though we could never know the phone contents in their entirety, we could still hear his half of the conversation.

Let his mistake of speaking about sensitive information be a lesson to all of you who casually use those secret service head pieces to talk about the intimacies of your everyday life while walking down busy city sidewalks. Even though you're not talking to me, I can still hear you! And quite frankly, I don't care who gave "it" to you and whether or not "the ointment" is working as directed!

For dear Chad Parker, I guess the habitual ritual of how he answers the phone was simply too hard to break even for someone so concerned about keeping his identity a secret from us. For a second I even felt kind of bad that he slipped up and that I found out his name even though he didn't want me to. But then I thought, "Who the hell answers the phone using their entire name?"

For the remainder of the drive I was in panic. Not over Chad Parker, but over Kate. A few minutes in the car had seemed like hours with the thought of Kate losing her stomach all over his well kempt back seat. We finally reached the end of the construction zone on the South end of Charleston, South Carolina. I casually mentioned to Chad (without addressing him by his name) that his hospitality had been greatly appreciated and that he could drop us off anywhere, but he insisted on taking us off the route and toward the shoreline.

"Downtown Charleston is a really happening place. You all will really enjoy yourselves there."

I didn't care too much about enjoying myself at the moment. My only concern was getting Kate out of this car and next to a trashcan. Given the circumstances, I suppose even the trashcan was an optional novelty. I would have settled for a storm-drain next to the curb. Either way, we were soon downtown and next to the shoreline. Chad pulled over next to a war memorial park of sorts and popped the trunk. I only assume that the park was of the war memorial variety because of its excess of cannons and men on horses.

Kate hobbled to a bench and waved good-bye while Rebecca and I shook hands with Chad Parker favorably. During the good-bye, I noticed myself smiling a lot in light of the intimate wisdom I had gained about this peculiar man who hadn't meant to reveal his name. I was so overjoyed, but I didn't dare let on that I had caught his name during his phone conversation for fear that the excitement would come to an end if he knew about his blunder. Knowing the name Chad

Parker was a privilege that I was not ready to share so readily, not even with Chad Parker himself.

As Rebecca and I headed toward the bench where Kate was recovering, Chad Parker called me back.

"Here," he said as he reached into the trunk. He pulled out a cylindrical tube about a foot and half long, handed it to me. Then he drove off.

By the time I walked the twenty feet to the bench where Kate and Rebecca were resting, the myth that had been Chad Parker had disappeared like the morning mist rising off the lake.

"What did he give you?" One of them asked as I approached the bench.

"I don't know. He said we could sell them in the parks here at night. Apparently there's some art festival here this weekend."

I opened the box and was confused by what I had found. The three of us looked quizzically at each other and then at the 500 small, neon-green sticks that spilled out onto the grass.

"Who was this guy?" We asked.

Well, we weren't entirely sure. The one thing we did know was that the secretive insurance salesman Chad Parker had just given us 500 of those tiny green glow sticks that most people only find at rave parties.

# Bohemian Weather Gear

About halfway through the trip I had to fly out West for ten days to take care of some personal business. The prospect of me leaving for a short time brought floods of emotions and heavy questions forward for all three of us. Looking back, it wasn't really all that big of a deal, but my departure caused ripples in two major areas. First, what did this mean for the legitimacy of the trip? Did my short withdrawal somehow disqualify me as a committed advocate? Did our efforts cause less of an impact if only two as opposed to three of us were traveling? In hindsight, I now realize that these types of questions are easily answered through a resounding "no." Plain and simple, taking personal time is forgivable and acceptable for anyone doing social justice work and I had an engagement that was important on multiple levels. So with the support of Kate and Rebecca, I took time away from the walk.

However, the second question that came to mind was completely gendered and socially constructed. How would the two women do walking and camping in unfamiliar areas unaccompanied by a male? Before my activism goes up in flames right on these pages, let me say that I can hear the sexism leaking from my question. I admit that sometimes balancing my practical choices with my perfect ideals is an imperfect struggle. Just because I wish to live in a world free from patriarchal domination does not mean that the reality has manifest and that I can fully ignore situations where danger happens based on gender. For example, I would absolutely love it if my two sisters could roam the earth and explore every nook and cranny at their own free will and, in truth, they can. Unfortunately, on their journey they are likely to encounter men that have been taught that they can take what they want from women. And because of this, fair or not, I hold onto the urge to be their protector. I know it's gendered, but sometimes I choose to make practical choices in the moment at the cost of marginalizing my hopes for the future.

Whatever the arguments are surrounding sexism and feminism, I'm glad I left the trip to more clearly articulate the fact that we are still operating within a culture that restricts the movement of women's bodies based on time and space. Sometimes these restrictions are physical, but other times these restrictions are also psychological and emotional.

When it comes to placing our patriarchal restrictions on women, culture is constantly policing females about where to go and what to avoid. Similarly, we create restrictions about the female body in terms of dress and wardrobe. Women's bodies are manipulated and distorted all in the hopes of pressuring them to contort in just the right manner to appease the male desire. In addition to the exceptionally problematic nature of manipulation and representation, the dehumanization of women also results in very real dangers women are threatened with. All of these physical and psychological restrictions thus lead to further objectification and makes it easier for men to physically hurt women because men no longer see women as people, but rather as objects.

A few years ago in an empty classroom on my college campus, this process of objectification was brilliantly described to me using a chair. Without disclosing what knowledge I was to learn from the lesson he was about to present, the other man in the room approached a chair and began speaking to it.

"Why hello chair," he said.

The chair didn't answer and remained still at the front of the room.

The man went on, "Um, excuse me chair. Do you mind if I sit on you?"

Peculiar questions of motive and insanity began to race through my mind. What kind of question was this for a chair? I mean, you either sit on the chair or you don't. The chair has no way of communicating and therefore, no way of objecting.

After repeating the question several times and patiently waiting for a response from the chair, the man finally sat in the chair and attempted to get comfortable for a good minute or so. Then finally he asked me, "What did you learn?"

"What? That was it? I was supposed to learn something from you talking to a chair?"

There was a pause and then a conversation unfolded about what may prove to be one of the most intelligent lessons on objectification I have ever heard.

"I talked to the chair and you probably thought this was crazy."

"Yes. Yes, I did," I responded, "But only because *it is* crazy."

"Well, it is only crazy because the chair is an object and not a person. I can sit in the chair, lean on the chair, or completely abuse the chair with no remorse or objection from society because that's what a chair is meant to do."

I was still confused, but becoming more and more intrigued. He continued.

"But, what if I treated a woman the way we treat chairs? We touch women, make sexual advances towards women, and abuse women everyday without asking. Do we not ask women for their input because we feel 'that is what they are meant to do?' Is it because we feel it is our right to treat them as objects? As sex objects? Instead, what if we all tried to communicate with women the same way I just tried to communicate with this chair?"

The man was a genius. Our culture has restricted and manipulated women's bodies to fit the needs of men without ever asking for any input from women. Some may say this type of logic will stain my reputation as a feminist and self-hating male, but I reject any and all consideration for membership within a movement. If my actions and rhetoric fit the template for feminism, or any other social theory, then those who wish to label me may label me as such. As for me, I simply see myself as just one guy who thinks that people should be asked about the use of their bodies instead of having other people making decisions about their bodies for them.

When it comes to walking the East Coast, whatever your opinion may be on the safety concerns of males and females traveling together or separate (and I'll be the first to agree that those concerns are valid and legitimate for most people in different ways), Kate and Rebecca succeeded in not getting hurt or killed despite my absence.

When I met back up with them in Richmond, Virginia, I found Kate first just South of downtown. We chatted for a bit about how things had been going over the last week because we had not talked since I left. I suppose this was a normal reaction. After being in contact with the same person day in and day out, you just take a break and don't even think about getting in touch. Kate and I walked for about a mile and then I started to fall back and wait for Rebecca. Rebecca was always the slowest, but I'll just attribute that to her weakness for aesthetics in scenery.

All of us finally met back up at a grungy gas station in downtown Richmond where a local paper was going to interview us. The interview was rather awkward and confusing, but we were in a position that required us to take any exposure for the issue that we could get. By the time the interview was done, it was about six o'clock and we were ready to find some food and some shelter.

Being in a college town, Richmond seemed like an easy place to get a bed for the night. We walked around downtown for a while talking with several locals about their suggestions, but no one really had much of an answer. The best we could get was the location of the firehouse and the police station. We went to the police station first and went over the same formalities of our journey that we had been telling for almost 50 nights now. However, our story seemed to spark very little interest with the officer on duty and he kept replaying our story back to us with a hint of skepticism and confusion.

"So let me get this straight," the officer said, "you've just been walking up to people and they've been giving you a place to stay?"

"That's the gist of it."

"Have you been to the police before?"

"Only a couple of times."

"And…"

"They usually can get us in touch with a church or a shelter."

His big dark eyes stared us down in a painful indifference.

"Well, I don't know what to tell you. The only place I know is a hotel three miles outside of town by the bus station."

We all looked at each other in a panic. There was no way we were willing to make a three mile hike off our route to some shady hotel next to a bus station at this time of night.

Rebecca interjected, "Can't you just put us up here? It looks like you have enough room."

The officer looked her over as if she was crazy, "The only way you can stay here is if you're locked up for a crime."

Then Rebecca said what proved to be the stupidest thing Kate or I heard the entire trip, "What if I told you there was a bomb in my backpack?"

As we were ushered out of the police station and into the rain, Rebecca was still laughing at her little joke. With Kate and I unamused, Rebecca promised that we would both look back and realize how funny she had been. To this day, I am still waiting for her to make good on that promise.

The rain was coming down hard and we had no place to go. With no other options, we decided to start walking towards the hotel next to the bus station. We stayed close to each other as we walked. Right behind me I could hear Rebecca still gabbing about the hilarity of her joke. We kept our eyes open for a taxi or bus that was headed in our direction, but none came.

Wet and tired, we reached the West side of downtown before having to turn North for the remaining two miles. In a fit of anger and frustration Kate stopped for a moment to vent, but her venting was interrupted by one of the most beautiful things I had ever heard. It was jazz. I snapped my head around and spotted the neon lights of a small bar across the street. Pouring out from the inside of its shanty walls was jazz music that could lift the spirit of any travelers down on their luck. The jazz music that came out from behind the neon glow breathed new life into me and helped me forget about Rebecca's slip-up at the police station and the rain that was currently flooding my only possessions.

We crossed the street and entered the crowded bar, gear and all, not caring about the fact that we needed rest and a place *to* rest. We search for a table in the back so that we could have a little room for storing our things. I suppose our thinking was that if we couldn't find shelter, then we could at least find peace for a few hours in the back of a bar listening to jazz music.

The waiter came over and asked the obvious question.

"What in the world are the three of you doing?"

His lighthearted sarcasm and kind mannerism put me at ease and I felt at home under the dim yellow light the hung gently above our table. As the night wore on the jazz music began to move slower and slower. It was as if the music was playing in sync with my emotions. Fast and furious fits of anger soon became a slow tempo of calm relaxation. It was that kind of relaxation where you give up the reins and just accept your situation. Right now, it was just best to live in the moment instead of worrying about the unknown events that lay before us.

We probably stayed in that bar for at least three hours before the thought of shelter entered our minds again. By now it was almost midnight and the heavy rains had slowed to a light shower. The band had trickled down to where only two of its members were still crammed in the corner opposite the front door. We decided it was best to get moving again and worked our way to the front bar.

As we were leaving, a woman named Jane followed us into the street and asked what we were doing and where we were going. When we got to the part about walking up to an unknown hotel in an unknown area, she interrupted.

"No way! I have a friend that lives just around the corner, you all can stay with her."

It seemed kind of odd that Jane was offering up the home of her friend who she hadn't yet spoken to or even knew that we existed, but Jane's bohemian look gave me confidence that the company she kept was always open to strangers crashing at their homes. She made a quick phone call and within minutes she informed us that everything was set, but that her friend wouldn't be back until the bars closed at 2:00 am. Until then we were content with just hanging around the bar and meeting all the folks Jane was there with, which seemed to be everybody – including the band.

We woke up rather early the next morning for spending a late night at the bar, but I was surprisingly refreshed. My guess is that my refreshment was somehow linked to the hospitality of others. If we were all just a little nicer to one another we may find folks in a better mood come 7:00 am. What was especially nice about waking up where we did was that we weren't completely out of the way of our route, which we would have been if we had made the trek all the way to that awful hotel. Instead, I woke up amidst a heap of blankets and sleeping bags on some kind stranger's floor while Kate and Rebecca were cozied up in a bed.

The woman who owned the place, who I met briefly before passing out amongst her living room belongings, had already left for work by the time I came to. So as a replacement for of waking up to conversations with our host, I went into the kitchen and found a simple note that told us to eat our fill and wished us well. I can't say that I was surprised by her generosity and carefree lifestyle – people like her were becoming common in our travels – but I can't hide my amazement with the trust she had just given to complete strangers who now inhabited her vacant home.

After eating, brushing my teeth, and packing my things, I slowly cracked opened the door to where Kate and Rebecca were sleeping in order to gently wake them up as I had done many times before. While I left a thankful response on the kitchen note, Kate and Rebecca went through their morning rituals of eating, brushing their teeth, and packing their things. As we checked the locks and closed the door behind us, we were greeted by the bright sun and damp air of a morning that was elegantly recovering from the previous evening's rainstorm.

# Expensive Shades
# and Reusable Drinks

**O**ur night in Richmond, Virginia was just the start of what was soon to be the most social week of the entire walk. After that first night in a bar, we logically deduced that frequenting bars may be useful in getting us some help along down the road, especially on Friday and Saturday nights. Remembering the first not-so-charitable church in Florida, it seems comical that we were now actively searching out bars as well as churches. When looking for help, I think we all just realized that sometimes we had better odds at bar counters than at pulpits. If that isn't a revelation about where God spends God's time, then I don't know what is.

A couple of days into this experiment of frequenting more bars, we found ourselves at the literal crossroads of civilization. With no place to go, churches or bars, we sat down in front of a gas station and relaxed in the shade of the setting sun. We hadn't been sitting there for any more than five minutes when a car pulled up in front of us and offered to take us to a local religious rally. Apparently there was a revival going on and as much as I have always wanted to see one of those events in action – all the healing, snake handling, and speaking in tongues – I just couldn't justify the five mile ride West not knowing where we were going to end up. I know it's unfair and the images that floated through my mind were completely stereotyped, but the thought of going actually freaked me out. I mean, we were already in the middle of nowhere and now someone wanted to take us out to a religious rally in the middle of a cornfield? I was content with taking my chances sleeping under the awning of this gas station.

With no other options, we started heading East toward the interstates. That was one great thing about our route. For the most part, there was always an interstate nearby, which usually meant a hotel or two. Since we had been couch surfing for the last week we found no harm in splurging a few bucks for our own room and a nice shower. Plus, a hotel meant sleeping in and free continental breakfast. We started in on the mile or so walk and soon saw the blue lights of a Hampton Inn peaking up above the horizon. Now the Hampton Inn was rather classy for our budget, but we figured it couldn't be that expensive given its location and the high probability of vacancy.

We entered the lobby and I was utterly surprised by the decadent furnishings. For a Hampton Inn, this place was quite lavish. By now we had done some under the table research and found that Kate was the best spokes-person when it came to wheeling and dealing. She created this sad look of innocence that made her pleading more adorable than my rugged beard and she could throw her voice into a whisper of effeminate and soothing vibrations, which trumped Rebecca's more aggressive and demanding approach. So Kate moved towards the front desk while Rebecca and I settled into the darkened corners of the lobby. We felt it best if our images remained inconspicuous.

I could hear the conversation from just behind the Romanesque columns that broke up the lobby. The voice of the man at the desk was pleasant and helpful and it sounded as if he was really trying to help Kate out. Rebecca and I cautiously made our way toward him, trying not to frighten or disturb our new friend. We didn't want any sudden movements to disrupt his sincerity.

With all three of us at the counter now, the man had finally disclosed the shocking fact that the best rate he could give us, including all the discounts, was $150 per night. A look of defeat stretched across our faces. Noticing the pain, the man picked up the phone and placed a call.

"Yes, I think that will work. I'll send them over now," he said to the anonymous figure on the other end of the receiver. It was as if we were being passed around through the secret service. We never knew what was going on, but we always knew that our best interest was their top priority.

He looked back at us, "That was the Day's Inn. They can give you a room for $70 a night."

Our savior had defied the rules of capitalism and had passed our business on to the competition. It was unconventional, but it was much appreciated. We headed out of the lobby and toward the Day's Inn that was up the road and across the street, hidden behind some fast food chains and overgrown trees.

We hadn't taken two steps out of the parking lot of the Hampton Inn before two men ran up behind us yelling for us to wait up. I spun around quickly not knowing what to expect. I mean, people calling out behind you could mean any number of things from "they need help" to "they want to cause you trouble.'

"Hey," one of them started, heaving to get air back into his deflated lungs, "we heard you all in the lobby talking to the receptionist about your situation." His pace had slowed and he had regained composure, "Listen, we're in town for a convention and we each have our own room with an extra bed. If you want, you can stay here with us for free. We don't mind. The company's paying for it."

Earlier in the walk, we all decided on a code that would let the other two know if we were uncomfortable with a situation; mainly the situation of spending the night with strangers either in their homes or in a room at the Hampton Inn. Actually, the Hampton Inn didn't come up specifically, but it seems relevant now. If a person creeps us out, we would simply talk to the others using fake names that made us sound country, such as Bobby Joe or Mary Sue. This would let the others know that something didn't feel right and we would simply respect their wishes and decline the offer no matter how we may feel about the situation as a democracy. In respect to someone else's comfort, I think empathy should always outweigh democracy.

Up until now, we also had time to sort out the creeps from the non-creeps through prolonged evaluation. This was made possible because we were usually engaged in a conversation with them for a while before they offered us a place to stay. But here we were standing in the parking lot outside the Hampton Inn with two grown men we have yet to say a word to and they're inviting us to stay the night *in their hotel room*. I think the initial shock was paralyzing and so we all just looked at each other unsure of who was going to take the lead – unsure who was going to start throwing around the Bobby Joes and Mary Sues. Surprisingly, no one did, and instead we just shrugged our shoulders and said, "Okay."

With the five of us sitting at the bar in an Applebee's a few doors down from the hotel, the three of us walkers soon found out that Mike and Greg were shades and blinds salesmen and installers from Jacksonville, Florida. We listened to their wild stories while they gave us the most complete lecture on selling window décor that I never wanted to know about. And I was completely fascinated.

Mike and Greg had been traveling around the world selling and installing shades for some of the richest people in the world who apparently had nothing else better to do with their money. And there was no shame about it. Even Mike and Greg, whose livelihood rested on the fact that some idiot would throw thousands of dollars at them for unnecessary furnishings, were open about how ludicrous their business was. But their philosophy was "someone's going to get paid to do it and it might as well be me." And they were good at what they did. These two had been flown into Russia to install blackout shades equipped with an astronomical clock for a man who wanted his shades to open with the rising sun every morning. They had traveled to California to set up a sound system that play Nickelback's "Rock Star" every time some pathetic rich guy with a macho complex walked in his front door. All this talk about timers and lights and soundtracks and clocks were mesmerizing and Mike and Greg's whole sale's angle was that they could do anything a customer could dream up.

At the end of the night we walked, some of us stumbled, back to the hotel and were looking to turn in quickly because we had to get up early due to Mike and Greg's early morning conference schedule. For safety reasons, the three of us decided to stay in the same room, Mike's room, even though there would have been a bed for all of us if we would have split up. Kate got into the shower while Rebecca made up the bed for the two of them. I piled up some linen on the floor for myself. As we were getting ready for bed, Mike casually asked us if we smoked as he lit up by the window of the non-smoking room. Curiously, Rebecca asked, "Cigarettes?" As Mike spun around in the office chair, the smell of freshly lit reffer enter my nostrils as he replied, "I wouldn't have asked if I only meant cigarettes." In any other setting these circumstances may have been weird, but judging by the events of the last few weeks, this situation now seemed fairly normal.

The next morning at 6:30 am, the four of us met up with Greg in the lobby for continental breakfast before we left. Apparently he was supposed to come back to our room and smoke some of Mike's stash, but he had passed out once he made it to his room. We left the Hampton Inn that morning and all we could do was recite the ridiculous stories we had experienced the night before. Those stories that were born out of our common experience – no matter how weird the experience – kept us walking in-step with each other that entire next day. This was something we hadn't done since those first few days in South Florida.

Little did we know that after leaving the Hampton Inn that morning, our good fortune would continue the rest of the way through the Commonwealth of Virginia. That very afternoon while walking through the middle-of-nowhere, we stopped at a gas station to grab some drinks and a few snacks for dinner. We hadn't been there very long and weren't planning for a long break, but as we were waiting for Rebecca to finish using the restroom, which was attached to the side of the building, a man approached Kate and I and asked what we were up to.

"Right now were looking for a place to stay. Do you know of anything around here?"

Scratching his head the man replied, "Well, there's not much if you're heading North for another 15 miles, but you can stay at my house if you'd like."

Without so much as a hesitation, Kate and I jumped at the opportunity. People like this man, Brian, always amaze me. In fact, people like this had become such a staple in our journey that my faith in the kindness of strangers has been completely rebuilt. For instance, there was this newlywed couple in Pompano Beach, Florida who took us in last minute after our original host came home an angry drunk, partnered Professors Jane and Roger who chased us down as we were leaving this Italian joint in Boca Raton after they had noticed our socially conscious t-shirts, and Marty and Chip who were artists on display at the Spoleto Festival in Charleston, South Carolina who would have adapted us if given the chance. Then there was Holly and Tom who responded to a National Organization for Women email and agreed to put us up for a night in central Florida, Janet in Melbourne who dropped us off at a hotel after buying us smoothies and then snuck back into the hotel and paid for it after we had already checked into our room (she never left a number and we never got to thank her – thank you Janet), and Ingrid from Mount Pleasant, South Carolina who took us in for two days of beach parties and cookouts with her son and dear friend Lidia after meeting us at her church service one Sunday morning. And I shouldn't forget to mention the ticket agents at such places as the Charleston Aquarium, Astronaut Hall of Fame, and various movie theaters, who let us in for free when we needed to get out of the mid-day sun and be entertained for a couple of hours.

This is just the short list. There were so many individuals along the way who bought us meals, gave donations, took us in, or put us up, that it would be nearly impossible to list them all. But I do want all of them to be recognized as the true journeymen and journeywomen of this trip. Without their help along the way, this trip would have been exponentially more difficult and, in all probability, unachievable.

As for Brian, we had literally been in contact with this individual for less than 30 seconds and already he was opening up his home to us. He didn't need to know anything about us. He didn't even know why we were walking. Hell, he didn't even know our names. All he knew is that we needed help. What surprised me even more about Brian, as opposed to people like Mike and Greg, was that Brian had four kids in his car and a wife at home who had no idea we were coming over for dinner and a sleepover.

Brian and his wife, Carrie, were those "cool" parents that everyone always wanted in high school. Carrie didn't even flinch when we walked in the door of their extravagant home and Brian announced that three complete strangers were going to stay the night with their four children in the house. Her only real reaction was a friendly smile with a sassy response of, "Well, I guess we'll have to make more room at the table."

At dinner we talked about everything from Brian's crazy hair style to religion. Brian's hairstyle, at the moment, was a spotted collage of pinks and purples that said, "Look at me! I'm young and hip despite this 40 year old body!" His story behind the hair was that a friend of his did hair and that he allowed her to experiment on his head however she felt fit. His philosophy was that she was the expert on hair so she should know what would look best on his head. Fair enough.

The conversation on religion was as equally as interesting. Brian and Carrie were very spiritual people who had deep ties to faith, yet they were never pushy with their beliefs in ways we had experienced numerous other times on the walk (which was a relief because even when we all proclaimed faith and agreed with those nagging evangelicals, there were still some people who would keep preaching to us as if they didn't believe we were telling the truth). Carrie was a Catholic and Brian had converted to Catholicism a few years after they had gotten married. Their children on the other hand, who were sixteen, fourteen, eight, and six, had "not yet decided on which religion they were going to follow." I could barely believe what I had just heard and had to replay it over and over again in my head until I understood. I was completely in awe. What kind of Catholic family leaves the religious decisions up to a six year old? But in hindsight, it makes a lot of sense. You can't really force your children into religion. And forcing them to partake in a religion that they have no interest in or real knowledge of does not do much except make them despise you and everything you stand for. Maybe the best solution as a parent is to just live your religion to the best of your abilities and hope that your kids want to model their lifestyle after yours. After all, it seemed to be working for this family. Brian did mention that his oldest, non-pressured, sixteen year old son was about to make a serious profession of faith.

We spent two days at Brian and Carrie's home before they took us into Fredericksburg, Virginia. It wasn't but a few miles away and Brian had some connections to the local women's centers in the area because he volunteered there as a computer technician. After hopping around to a couple of different offices and then visiting some of the women who were currently living at the shelter, Brian and Carrie dropped us off downtown where we were left on our own to figure out the rest of the day.

By now it was late afternoon and we didn't want to move out of the city, so we decided to find a place where we could grab a late lunch a possibly meet up with some folks who were willing to take us in for the night. Besides, it was Kate's 21st birthday and Rebecca and I wanted to be sure that she enjoyed herself. We found a nice little bar and grill and went up stairs to relax in a more casual environment. I don't know whether it was luck or fate, but either way, we hadn't been there more than a few minutes before the lounge started to fill with customers from all sorts of professions who were just getting off of work. We would come to find out that we were stuck in the monthly meeting area of an organization called Green Drinks.

Green Drinks was an organization that consisted of all sorts of people whose main concern was eco-friendly everything. What appealed to me most about this organization was that it helped people tackle eco-problems from every different angle. Whether you were a lawyer, a construction worker, a teacher, a cab driver, or a college student, everyone was welcome and could attend, get advice, and exchange ideas about how to make various career paths "greener." The best way I could describe the atmosphere at Green Drink was that it was a place where good people were able to network with mentors who were willing to share their success stories. In a way, I was almost envious of these folks' relationships since the three of us had only a handful of role models to look up to and model our walk after. Furthermore, and to my continuing disappointment, many people I have met in field of social justice are protective of their work and don't share their ideas for fear of copyright infringement. The folks at Green Drinks, however, understood the usefulness of their work and this was refreshing. Their concerns were more focused on dispersing their materials as opposed to gaining financial compensation for them. In essence, social transformation was at the center of their concerns rather than profit – imagine that.

To make things even more exciting, local newspapers and bloggers often attended Green Drinks and with the buzz that slowly began to circulate about us, it was evident that a few people were aching to get our story. Once all of interviewing with the press was over, I finally got the opportunity to meet the Green Drinks leader himself, Dan Dukes.

Judging by his name and his mustache, my first inclination was that he was in the adult entertainment business. I don't think my assumption was that far fetched seeing that some adult stars are probably "green" and may be attending these meetings. However, I soon learned that I had been mistaken and that Dan Dukes was actually one of the leading men in Virginia who did eco-conscious construction work. Dan and I hit it off immediately over the finger food buffet and he ecstatically informed me that I was allowed to do anything I wanted to do that night at Green Drinks.

"Excuse me Dan," I inquired, "Is this food for everyone or just members?"

"Man!" Dan boasted, "You can do whatever the fuck you want man!"

I was a little taken back by the unnecessary profanity and the volume at which it was shouted, but I soon grew attached to Dan's presence and the way in which he showed his affection.

"Man!" Dan yelled again, "Don't ask any more questions. After what you all did walking here from Miami, you..." he stuck his finger into my chest, "...can do whatever the fuck you want!"

I was really getting to like Dan. He was like that weird uncle who got stuck in the seventies and your parents only allowed you to see him on holidays in order to cut down on the influence he could have on their otherwise level-headed children. Like most other large gatherings that we accidentally stumbled into, Green Drinks allowed us to give a presentation about ourselves before they got into the scheduled events of the evenings. Actually, we didn't even ask if we could give a presentation because Dan pretty much forced us up onto the stage. We gave the same formatted speech we have given countless times before and this particular presentation must have gone well because a few months later I received an email from Dan Dukes stating that we won an annual Green Drinks award for activism as voted on by the members. So that was pretty cool.

The rest of the evening was full of political discussions that became more and more conspiracy oriented as people became more and more intoxicated. Bars are funny like that, especially when frequented by political activists. People start off normal with casual bantering about Republicans verses Democrats, but by the end of the night, the government has made a deal with Nike to put sensors in shoes so that they can track everyone with a new pair a Jordan's. Actually, now that I think about it, it doesn't seem that far fetched. In all, I think the conversations mixed with an energetic crowd, live music, and plenty of dancing, made for a very nice birthday celebration for Kate. It was almost as if Green Drinks had planned this whole night around her. I think she earned it.

We finally left Green Drinks at one o'clock and headed home with this lovely woman named Jeanne whose crazy socialite mother had brought her there to meet people because she didn't think it was okay for her single, 30-something year old daughter to live in a big house all by herself and work long shifts as a doctor, which she had to report for at seven o'clock that morning. The three of us, on the other hand, were picked up by Jeanne's mom at around nine o'clock and she drove us back into downtown Fredericksburg where we were dropped off at the bar that had hosted all the festivities the night before. Waving goodbye and thanking her for the ride, we turned Northbound and started walking – one foot in front of the other.

# Cultural Indifference

With so many days behind us, I was constantly reminded of how many days we still had ahead of us. I suppose this sort of sentimental afterthought is a lot like how life is. You know, living in this constant state of obtainable goal after obtainable goal. Most of us rushed through the first 18 years of life trying to get that high school diploma thinking that life would be cozy once that feat was tackled. Approaching college, many of us repeat this mindset only to learn that what awaited us on the other side was work, maybe some more school, and the added bonus of bills. What we usually fail to realize is that at every age we are living real life and rushing through these experiences only gets us in the ground that much faster – and a little more out of breath.

The walk often teased me like this. Crossing one state line felt so great for about a mile and a half and then the realization would set in that I was at the Southern edge of just another state and I needed to walk to its Northern border. And while strolling past the Mason-Dixon did give me a reassuring feeling that we were only a few big-city hops away from reaching Boston, the truth was that almost a third of the trip still remained. Besides the drained enthusiasm and pain felt everywhere throughout my body, we would also soon discover that the Northern part of the walk would prove to be our biggest battle against cultural indifference to our message.

The next time you pull out a map of the United States, one thing you should notice about the East Coast is its highly populated Northern half and mostly rural Southern half. A gentleman in Maryland even informed us that a third of the United States population lives in this upper-third of the East Coast within a few hundred mile radius. Unfortunately the cruel lesson for us was that upon exiting Virginia, most people on our route seemed to stop caring about our message no matter its social, political, or moral intentions. I suppose that's fair enough. I mean, with all of the small-town-living in the South, it's expected that a trio of teal shirted walkers would draw attention to themselves fairly easily. If not for their unusual outfits, then at least for the fact that nobody knows who they are. And from everything I can gather, people in small towns get to know their neighbors and visitors whether they want to or not.

Yet this sort of attention seeking logic proves almost useless in big Northern cities because all sorts of people are dressing crazy and hardly anybody seems to know anybody else anyhow. Arguably, big cities are constructed in a way to allow people to inconspicuously fade into the small cracks of a culture which is so monstrous in numbers that it can't be bothered by the disappearance or addition of just one or two of its members. Therefore, seeing a stranger who looks strange is normal and expected. In fact, in a city of several hundred thousands, it is big news the day you *do* run into someone you know.

All of this leads to our dilemma North of Virginia, which was the hard life lesson of realizing that nobody cared about our walk anymore. Of course I am speaking in a slightly dramatic form and of course there were a *few* people here and there who raised interest, but collectively the cities were a wash. In addition, a lot of folks up North caused us the exact opposite problem we had with a lot of folks in Southern Florida. In Southern Florida, folks didn't think that we would make it. Up North, folks didn't believe that we had done it.

Once we reached the metro areas of Washington D.C., it just became one big city after another full of uninterested locals and uninterested local media. Washington D.C., Baltimore, Philadelphia, New York – all of these cities had major media outlets, and none of them took interest in our otherwise exciting and important mission to travel eighteen-hundred-miles by foot in order to bring awareness to sexual violence. In fact, it was so difficult and depressing that there were times when I no longer even cared about finishing the walk and could have easily hopped on a train and relaxed for the last couple of weeks visiting the various museums and historic landmarks these cities offered. I may have well enjoyed their usefulness while I was there, but then I was reminded that finishing this walk wasn't about me and that as much as I didn't want to be there for the last few weeks to face the overwhelming indifference of the big cities, survivors of sexual violence never want to be in their position either. And most of them have to deal with the indifference on a daily basis for the rest of their lives, rather than just for a few weeks as a privileged white male trying to do some good in our world.

When I can't immediately change a situation or the attitudes of the people in that situation, I often try to come up with little theoretical explanations that at least help me break it down logically so that I can have some peace in better understanding the situation. The explanation I came up with in those last few weeks of walking was that cultural indifference is the end result of the patriarchal systems that perpetuate violence against women in the first place. In short, because I am a man I have the privilege of being indifferent to sexual violence against women if I want to be because the problem isn't a problem that directly affects my everyday way of living. Why would any man want to make sexual violence an issue in his already hectic life? Yes, there are men who are survivors of sexual violence, and their stories should not be minimized, but collectively men *are not culturally threatened* with being sexually violated. In contrast, women are disproportionately sexualized in our culture and therefore, have more reason to fear the sexually violent acts created through objectification. Furthermore, as a man I can desensitize myself to sexual violence and mentally make it an issue that affects "other" people I don't care about. Or, I can completely erase the problem of sexual violence from the forefront of my mind because I can choose to bury it beneath the heap of other life pressing issues, thus making sexual violence relatively invisible in my day-to-day operation.

Likewise, living in big cities is hectic and hard enough on a person. Why would people want to take on somebody else's problems? Because of the stress that comes with living in a big city full of social issues, it makes sense that some of the people who live there would have to desensitize themselves to the needs of "others" in order to survive the heartache that comes with investing in another person's troubles. There are of course people in the city who make it their life's work to solve social issues, and this is not to say that people in big cities wouldn't care if an issue was placed directly in front of them. For example, I think the aftermath of September 11th is the perfect representation of people pulling together in an *immediately* dire situation. But overall, and because of the vast amount of social issues rampant throughout cities on a *daily* basis, it would be grueling for a person to commit to eradicating every single one of them.

A large percentage of us, both rural and city, may dance around with a few issues here and there throughout our lives (for many that is linked to throwing spare change in a cup every once in a while), but most people rarely, if ever, make any strong commitments in terms of time, energy, and money. Unfortunately, because most people can't get involved with everything this also means that most people usually don't get involved with anything. In the end, sexual violence usually ends up getting buried beneath the heap of other pressing social issues such as homelessness, homicide, and homeland security.

When it comes to sexual violence, patriarchy affords men the privilege of indifference even though they are tied to the issue as the perpetrator almost 100 % of the time! Illustrated through indifference, we have become a culture that sees sexual violence as too overpowering, too insignificant, too complicated, or too costly a problem, and we render it an impossible issue to successfully eradiate. Because we cannot see the light at the end of the tunnel, we often become paralyzed and choose to do nothing instead of doing something. Or, we blame the victims by telling women to "act right" and all will be fine instead of *demanding that men are the ones who need to change their behavior.* Whatever excuses we have for our cultural indifference, sexual violence is real, it hurts, and it will not go away if we ignore it. We have to commit to doing something immersed and long-term.

In spite of the collective apathy, we chose to make the best of our stays between D.C. and Boston. D.C. was the first big city stop where we stayed with one of Rebecca's sorority sisters for a couple of days, which allowed us to visit all those historic landmarks I mentioned earlier. There was even a festival that was taking place along the National Mall so our day was filled with free samples and traditional Mexican music. On the way to Baltimore, Kate received a phone call from a friend of hers back home whose parents wanted to put us up in this fancy hotel on the harbor right next to the Oriole's stadium. To our relief, the staff at this hotel was extremely interested in our stories to the point where this large man named Alvin kept sneaking us free drinks and snacks through the hotel's room service.

On the way to Philadelphia, we made a unlikely detour to the harbor town of Elkton, Maryland after hearing about its incredible fireworks display that was put on every weekend leading up to the forth of July. Now detours were usually avoided and democratically voted against with little opposition, however, it was the forth of July weekend and the thought of grills and explosives was too tempting to pass up. I must say that I was quite pleased with the show put on by Elkton that night. Because of the various connections we had intentionally made throughout the day by seeking out some local politicians and city leaders, especially one Bob Gell who I am convinced pretty much runs the entire Northern seaboard, we were able to get a free room at a nearby hotel as well as a little media coverage, which hadn't happened since we left Fredericksburg.

Leaving the city of Elkton and Bob Gell behind, we high-tailed it out of Maryland and through Delaware in an attempt to reach Philadelphia for the calendar scheduled forth of July celebration. It was an exciting twist of fate that made it possible for us to reach Philadelphia for the United States' 232nd birthday. Originally, we were scheduled to be sandwiched somewhere between D.C. and Philadelphia for the forth, but thanks to a few short-cuts provided by our hosts throughout the trip, we were able to spend this forth of July with John Legend and few thousand of his closet friends in the city where the signing of our independence all went down.

The next big stop after Philadelphia was New York City and its massive suburb known as the state of New Jersey. Our first stop in Jersey was Camden where I met up with a few friends of mine at the local homeless shelter Frank's Place where I had worked for a year between undergraduate and graduate school. Next, we traveled up the side streets of Jersey staying close to the New Jersey turnpike and soon found ourselves in Trenton. Now I know Trenton is a rough area, but I wasn't too concerned because we were only traveling during the day and we had already been through plenty of tough towns like Baltimore and Camden. But when we stopped at a fire station at four o'clock in the afternoon looking for advice on a place to stay that night and a man stumbled in with stab wounds after being robbed for three dollars in bus fare, I was okay with the fire chief giving us a ride North to Lewisville.

From Lewisville we continued North through Princeton and all the bourgeois areas leading up towards Newark. In Princeton, we got lunch from some really nice realtors when they saw us outside their business with our faces pressed up against their glass window marveling over all the fancy homes they had on display. Who knows? I may be in the market for a million dollar home someday. When we finally did reach the Southern end of Newark, walking became every bit the mess we had expected. All the nice roads suddenly merged into unwalkable highways and interstates and we were content with grabbing a train in Elizabeth and heading over to Manhattan.

To be fair, walking through New York wasn't entirely necessary and we could have just as easily avoided it all together. Perhaps we would have even saved a few extra miles on our trip by circumventing through

Northern New Jersey. But we all had friends in NYC and it would have been a shame just to walk by the Big Apple and not experience it for a couple of days. Even with all of its crazy commotion and rushed people who never slowed down, New York City was good to us. Our hostesses Julie, Andrea, and Molly were all currently working in NYC and lived in Uptown Manhattan. Julie knew Kate from back home in Michigan, took us in, and allowed us to invade her space for a few nights as we toured the city.

Utilizing their apartment as an operational headquarters (kind of like the Bat-Cave) we ventured in NYC just like Sara Jessica Parker. Kate and Rebecca did a little shopping and drank a few cocktails in SoHo while I visited with some old friends, Jonathan and Will. Jonathan is a good friend of mine from high school who was currently dancing with a company out of NYC and Will and I had lived together in Camden during Mission Year. He was now interning with a local graphic design company in Brooklyn for the summer. At the end of it all, the three of us spent our last day playing in Central Park and left NYC feeling a little lighter on our feet. However, the lightness had little to do with the stress lifted from our shoulders and mostly to do with the amount money sucked out of us from the city. Seriously, who charges $4 for a bowl of Frosted Flakes?

As we were leaving NYC, I gained new knowledge about our geographic location that made the prospect of getting out of there even more worth while. Apparently NYC sits only a few miles South of the Connecticut border, which meant that we had only one more state to go before entering the final three day trek through Massachusetts to its capitol Boston. Now, in my mind Connecticut was a very small and wimpy state compared to well, let's say Florida, Georgia, South Carolina, or *any other state we had already been though*. However, after picking up and studying the new state map we bought at a local Walgreens near the New York/ Connecticut border, I soon realized how much psychological power that state would suck out of me. I know this seems a little exaggerated, but the reality of it was that our final test was to walk the longest possible distance through that freaking state! We were entering Connecticut at its Southwest corner and had to exit at its Northeast corner. My dreams of a nice leisurely walk had been crushed.

With this new revelation about the shape of Connecticut came some other sad news: Rhode Island was no longer going to be a stop on our journey through New England. Originally, I had suggested that because Rhode Island was just around the corner that we could travel straight East and then straight North to get to Boston and still be able to step foot in Rhode Island. Contrary to my previously held beliefs about distance and maps, our certified math genius Rebecca informed me about an ancient legend that involved some guy name Pythagorean and how diagonals were shorter than the sum of their two sides. Her "logic" won out, and we settled on cutting straight through the middle of Connecticut like a Miracle Blade through a ripe tomato.

As we were making our final steps out of New York over the Connecticut border late one evening, we found ourselves in yet another predicament. The sun had been set for at least an hour and we still had no shelter for the night. There wasn't even a hotel nearby. To add to our misery, our smell was offensive and it was difficult getting within an ear-shot of people on the street to explain what we were doing and our dire situation. With few options left, and tired feet, we did what any sensible college students would do in that desperate situation. We grabbed some Buffalo Wild Wings and went to a 10:30 showing of *Wanted*. We collectively agreed that *Wanted* was a good movie and now that I've mentioned it maybe I can finally get that meeting with Morgan Freeman, or maybe just a phone-call?

To make a long story short, we got out of the movie at 12:30 am, walked over the Connecticut border around 1:30 am, and finally found a hotel at 3:00 am. Okay, *we* really didn't find the hotel, but we did find nice men from Brooklyn at some gas station who were on their way to a fishing hole, and they gave us a ride to a hotel using their fancy GPS. So really the lady's voice on the GPS found the hotel. Either way, I'm just glad that those Southern Connecticut towns have

Ferrari, Lamborghini, and Porsche dealerships that are brightly lit up all night. My logical guess is that all of those lights are used as a device to deter theft, but my gut likes to think that all those rich folks in Port Chester and Greenwich were really looking out for us. Whatever the real case may be, I'd like to take this opportunity to personally thank Connecticut for all of those sidewalks and street lights.

# Who the Hell is Senator Dodd?

**A**s we walked through the hills of Connecticut, the hope and glory of our expedition had all but been sucked out of me. Frankly, I couldn't care less about what else happened on the trip. We had traveled for two and half months and we were less than two weeks from being done. I was happy that it was almost over. Not because raising awareness about sexual violence had become any less important, but because I was tired. I wasn't so much physically tired, I had gotten used to that, but the slow pace of the farmer's fields passing by had taken its mental toll.

We were now in central Connecticut and a few days back we had been interviewed by a small paper in Southwestern Connecticut. Being the tactful person that she is, Rebecca bluntly stated in the interview that the small town Southerners had been more hospitable than the big city Northerners, but that she still had hope in someone taking us in. This was perhaps her way of issuing a not so subtle plea for help. We had looked for this newspaper interview for a couple of days in the scheduled paper, but we never saw it and eventually had walked out of its distribution range. We were too depleted to even muster up any efforts of following up with the reporter in order to figure out if he had any intentions of actually running the piece. That's when Kate received a phone call.

Being the leader she was, Kate had made our website rather artful and full of information I would have never thought to include. If it was left up to me, I would have slapped together a one-page blog and forgotten all about it, but not Kate. Kate fancied that webpage up with mission statements, biographies, sponsors, office directory (which happened to be her dorm room), and media contact information. This was just in case someone needed to call us.

The phone call she received this particular day was from a woman named Jackie. Jackie explained that she had read about our walk in a Connecticut paper and because she was the wife of a Senator, she felt that it was her responsibility to show us some Connecticut hospitality. Because we were on foot and unfamiliar with Connecticut, it took us a while to figure out where we were in relation to Jackie's house. Eventually, we figured out that we were only about 20 miles North of her home. That first conversation between her and Kate ended briefly and lacked any critical details about schedules and rides, but Jackie assured us that she would call back later. Later of course being that arbitrary time slot for sometime in the future.

I was rather pessimistic about the whole conversation and I seriously doubted that Jackie would call back if it meant disrupting her daily schedule. From the sound of Kate's recollection, Jackie became hesitant when she realized that we had no way of coming to her and that she would have to come to us. We couldn't travel South, and 20 miles is an entire day on foot, 20 minutes in the car.

Against our better judgment, we decided to sit and wait for her phone call out of the hopes that she would pull through. By now it was the middle of the day and I felt anxious about stopping on a whim that Jackie might call back. After all, we still had plenty of mileage to cover before sunset and we weren't anywhere close to a town that provided adequate shelter. But in the end, our fatigue got the best of us and we decided to take rest under the shelter of an abandoned outdoor diner. From the looks of it, this diner had been out of service for a while. The outside walls held paintings of waitresses on roller skates and giant cheeseburgers with facial features. Also, the benches and picnic tables were collapsing so we were forced to sit on a curb with our backs up against the walk-up service window.

"Who is this lady again?" I asked

Kate sounded equally unsure, "I don't know. Some woman who says she's the Senator's wife."

"Like a State Senator?"

"I don't know. His name's Dodd. Do you know anyone name Dodd?"

We all shook our heads and retired to various activities to occupy ourselves while passing the time. Soon it had been about two hours since Jackie called and in between reading and napping, I decided to make a phone call.

"Dad, do know a Dodd from Connecticut?"

My dad knew Senator Chris Dodd all too well. Through his fast-paced talking I learned that Chris Dodd had been in the Senate for a long time and that he was a frequent guest on Sunday morning news shows and C-SPAN.

The moment I hung up the phone, I could see that Kate was also ending a conversation about Chris Dodd with her father. Kate's dad had looked up Chris Dodd on the internet and was reading his long list of accomplishments to her over the phone. The only conclusion I could reach about this Dodd character was that he had a lot of influence with banks.

Still skeptical of Jackie calling back and worried that we may have looked up information on the wrong Dodd, we continued to wait under the shade of that decrepit old diner. Finally, someone mentioned that they were hungry, which of course trigger a reflex in all our stomachs, so we walked a little ways down the road and stepped into a carry-out pizza joint to grab some lunch. We ended up eating the pizza straight out of the box and the owner was kind enough not to get irritated by the fact that we were chowing down in his store window. About the time we had finished off a large cheese pizza, Kate received another phone call.

It was Jackie. Trumping my doubts, she had pulled through! She had made arrangements with the Senator's personal assistant to come pick us up and drive us back to their home. When the car arrived, a nice looking future politician stepped out and greeted us. His name was Brian and he helped us load our belongings into the trunk of the small town car with the smile and charisma only a politician could fake. During the short 25 minute drive back, Brian filled our minds with stories and wonder of Christopher Dodd, the senior Democratic Senator from Connecticut.

As the car pulled into the driveway, I was surprised at how humble the house was. Not to say that is wasn't beautiful or immaculately kept, but just that it was a lot smaller and more approachable than I had anticipated. We would later find out that the Dodd's home was an old two-room school house complete with historic photographs and a working school bell whose rope still hung down into the middle of the living room. I thought that this was rather playful for a Senator.

Jackie Dodd greeted us cordially at the back door as Brian parked the car further up the driveway in an area that overlooked the river. Jackie would probably never admit it, but I have a heightened suspicion that she never expected the filth we brought with us and therefore, I commend her on her ability to remain both hospitable and pleasant even when being faced with the two and half months of the dirt and sweat that lined our shoes and equipment.

At the request of Mrs. Dodd, we left our equipment, shoes, and socks at the back door before she escorted us inside and began to recite our options for this evening's affairs. I was already ecstatic about getting a shower and dinner, and I wanted them in that order. After that, the possibilities for entertainment seemed endless and completely up to somebody else.

Because I didn't want to feel rushed, I offered to take my shower last. In hindsight, I never thought that taking a shower would be such an outlandish experience, but now I realize that taking a shower in a Senator's bathroom is like an adventure. It's not your average bathing experience. These showers contain moments of ecstasy. For one, this shower was a water lovers dream with two separate shower heads. One was a giant rainforest waterfall directly above the drain so that the water gently fell on you as opposed to being shot at you from an angle like some archaic means of hygiene. The second head flowed from the side to ensure that your ribs stayed well hydrated during the experience.

The other reason I enjoyed the shower so much was because it afforded the opportunity to accomplish yet another life goal. This goal being that I've always wanted to smell like a Senator. At this point in my life, I had never actually been close enough to catch the scent of a Senator, but based on my assumptions of the types of smells that must come with political power, fame, and fortune, I just assumed that the smell must be extraordinary and therefore, one that I too would someday wish to coat myself in. I was correct. The assortment of hygiene products in Chris Dodd's shower was absolutely breathtaking and superb. These bathing items were really top of the line. Intimidated as to which soap to use, I settled for the one I felt conveyed a certain sense of musk. You know, the kind of musk you expect a Senator to smell of.

After the unreasonably prolonged shower (and yes, I took my sweet, sweet time. I mean, how often do you get to shower like a Senator? In fact, the only shower I imagine could have topped this would be a shower taken in the White House, and I remain open to an invitation from President Barack Obama and First Lady Michelle Obama if they would like my company), I returned upstairs for a delicious family meal with Jackie and the kids. At dinner Jackie informed us that Senator

Dodd would be returning from Washington that night at around 10:00 pm and that meant that it was up to us to entertain ourselves for the next four hours.

As we continued to eat a variety of pasta dishes and warm butter rolls, Mrs. Dodd slipped away to make a phone call. When she returned she asked if any of us were interested in theatre. We all politely nodded in affirmation and she began explaining a night life possibility to attend a local theatre production.

"This is a real top of the line community theatre," she began, "It has been voted best community theatre in the nation several times. You know, it's not one of those cheap $30 or $40 a ticket community theatres."

Hold on. Was she really telling me that thirty or forty dollars a ticket is considered cheap for a community theatre production? Last time I checked, community theatre was being performed by soul-searching parents who sold insurance or taught chemistry at the local high-school and was being directed by glory-seeking folks who missed their chance to move out of the suburbs and risk it all in the big city.

Whatever their reasons for the outlandish pricing, it wasn't going to cost us a dime so we decided to attend the theatre and forgo the late night boat ride on the river. After making our decision, we quickly noticed how little time we had before the production began at 7:30. By seven o'clock we had finished eating our meal, but contrary to our instincts to go hurry up and get ready, Mrs. Dodd hastily rushed around the kitchen preparing our desert.

"There is strawberry, blueberry, or blackberry," she commanded, "and there's some ice cream in the fridge!"

We sat stunned at the table. We were unsure as to why she was bothering with dessert at such a late hour and why she was yelling fruit flavors at us from across the kitchen island, but she insisted that we eat it.

"Hurry over here," she went on.

We scrambled to the kitchen counter and began to enjoy our delicious desert over the kitchen sink. At 7:15, I had all but choked myself shoving the desert down my throat when Mrs. Dodd literally grabbed us all and rushed us down stairs. During this whole fiasco, she was continually ensuring us that there was plenty of time and that the theatre was only five minutes away.

Given the circumstances of our current situation, I found nothing wrong with what we were wearing. I mean, throughout the walk we respectfully maintained two sets of clothes. There was one for walking (gross) and one for resting (clean). Yet it was apparent that my clean khaki shorts and clean blue t-shirt were not quite dressy enough for the prestige community theatre that night. In all honesty, I wasn't concerned with someone there taking notice of our casual clothing, but Jackie Dodd would have none of our protest.

As we entered her and the Senator's bedroom on the lower level of the house, it suddenly occurred to me that our wardrobe was about to be attacked on the frontlines like a very bad reality television show. Kate and Rebecca were first. Frantically rummaging through her things, Mrs. Dodd began throwing shoulder-padded dresses and pant suits at the two. Catching whatever seemed to match, the two of them hysterically began changing into Mrs. Dodd's outfits while strewing their own clothes all over the bedroom floor. For those of you keeping track mentally, the answer is "yes," we all ended up changing in front of a Senator's wife.

Without immediately recognizing the fate that lay before me, I was next in her line of fire. As I tried to grasp what was happening, Mrs. Dodd flung open the closet doors of her husband and threw before me the fine clothing collection of Senator Christopher Dodd himself, the senior Democrat from Connecticut.

"You and my husband look about the same size," she casually remarked almost out of breath by now.

I was speechless and could not reply. What would I have said anyway? I was too busy rattling around the implication of stepping into the clothing of one of the most powerful men in the country to even try and reason with his flustered wife. First, she tossed me a shirt and jacket. The ensemble was a fine, navy-blue suit coat wrapped around a steam-pressed yellow shirt (which Brian probably laundered) and I, in one of my less tactful moments, rummaged through the pockets. I would like to say that this was in an effort to be sure that Mrs. Dodd didn't leave me with the gigantic responsibility of watching over the Senator's things. You know, one of those "if I don't have it, I can't be responsible for losing it" moments. But no, this would be far from the truth. What I really wanted to find in those pockets was some highly classified government…whatevers. Unfortunately, for me (fortunately for Dodd) nothing was there.

Next were the pants and the loafers. In all honesty, there was part of me that wanted to not wear pants at all and simply parade around the theatre halls in my boxers. How hilarious would it have been to make the front page news as the guy who was dressed from the waist up like the senior Democratic Senator from Connecticut and no pants? But I gave in. Partly out of respect for Jackie, but mostly out of respect for my parents who I'm sure didn't want me to be "that guy." So I clumsily threw on the pants while sliding my feet into the brown leather loafers – no socks (sorry Senator).

Leaving our clothes on the floor, we rushed out of the house and were into the car at 7:25. When I look back, I don't think I've gotten dressed so nicely in such a short amount of time since I was little and my parents were trying to rush four decent looking children off to church on Sunday morning. When we finally arrived at the theatre, we were greeted like royalty at the front door. It was evident that they were waiting for the guests of Mrs. Dodd. After formal, polite exchanges between Mrs. Dodd and the theatre crowd, we were briskly escorted to our seats.

We were shown to our seats by two lovely women and seated just in time for the lights to go dim and for the show to begin. Evident by the looks of a packed house, the seats we were sitting in had been held and were always on reserve. Who else could have gotten tickets to a sold out show 30 minutes before it began?

At intermission, a gentleman approached our seats and introduced himself as an important person who dealt with the theatre's personal affairs. I wish he could have been a little less wordy with his title and just said "public relations," but he was quite nice so I let it slide. I was, however, in awe at how he had memorized and recited all of our qualifications to be in the theatre that evening. Of course, the main reason was that Jackie Dodd had called him. He then went on to tell us how impressed he was with what we were doing "with all the walking and such." Not to diminish our accomplishments of the walk, I was fairly impressed myself, but I think he was more impressed that we were guests of Jackie Dodd, and it saddens me to admit that being her guest might actually have been a more impressive accomplishment for most folks. In fact, if I was pressured to only choose between the walk and knowing Jackie Dodd, I'm unsure of which accomplishment I would place on a résumé.

Either way, he concluded our formal introductions by politely inquiring about whether or not we would like some snacks. We graciously accepted by way of asking for bottled waters and over-priced chocolate bars. Before he left he told us to enjoy the rest of the show and informed us that we were to rendezvous in the Member's Lounge after the show. If I recall correctly, the Member's Lounge was a place for people to meet after the show who wore jackets with snappy-buttons on the collar. Thanks to Mrs. Dodd, I did have a jacket, but unfortunately, no snappy-buttons.

When the show completed, which by the way was brilliant and totally worth more than thirty to forty dollars a ticket, we were completely taken off guard and amiably humbled by what happened next. As the applause grew and the crowd stood in a standing ovation just before the final curtain dropped, the main actor approached center stage to make an announcement. Classy as this place was, I figured a celebrity must be in the audience.

"We have some special guests here with us tonight," he began, "There are three college students in the audience tonight who walked here all the way from Miami and are on their way to Boston to raise awareness about sexual violence."

At such an announcement, I lost my sense of reality and it began to sink in that nearly two-thousand people were standing and clapping for us. I suppose some were still clapping for the performance, I sure was, but I like to imagine that they were all clapping for us. As the people exited the auditorium, hundreds stopped to shake our hands, give us words of encouragement, and thank us for our persistence. There were even a few financial contributions that were slipped into my jacket pocket. When the crowd had finally died down, we were able to exit and, as directed, headed straight for the Member's Lounge. To my surprise, the Member's Lounge was a small room, but it did have wall-to-wall carpeting and fancy décor. And fortunately, snappy-buttons were not a requirement for entrance. To our astonishment, the gentleman who had given us the bottled water and expensive chocolate earlier was there waiting for us along with the show's lead actor and a camera!

"We were hoping that we could get a picture of you all with Peter for our newsletter."

Of course you could! After taking a few pictures we headed back to the Senator's home, which was only a short five or six blocks down the road. Along the way, the mood was joyous and we were all wound up like seven year olds on pixie sticks. We laughed and played through the dark roads and kept on asking, "what is happening?" and "who are we?" We couldn't believe our good fortune and the strange series of events that led up to this crazy night. I, for one, was still wearing the Senator's clothes and we joked at the prospect of now having to meet this guy. When we arrived back, we entered through the back door. Kate and Rebecca went in first and I patiently watched as they introduced themselves to Senator Dodd. When it was my turn, he grabbed my hand and lightheartedly said, "Nice outfit."

It was a moment for the history books. I had just met a Senator wearing his clothes.

Taking the winding staircase up to the kitchen, the three of us and the Dodd's had a few late night snacks around the dinning room table and engaged in some more personal conversation. Senator Dodd asked mostly about our upbringings, our families and I particularly remember him commenting on how proud my parents must have been to have all of their children in or finished with college.

The Senator humored us with some brief discussions about his political career, which was something I'm sure he's was tired of talking about, especially during introductions. We were also in awe of all the famous politicians he considers close friends and who he talks with everyday. After an hour or so of chit-chat, Mrs. Dodd finally called the conversation and we were all, including the Senator, tucked into bed.

Provided with fresh sheets and a cozy robe, I went to bed in the Senator's office. Rich with dark wood interior and shelves upon shelves of books, the office was actually a lot more diminutive than one might imagine. I took my time getting ready for bed by glancing through some of the titles that lined the book shelves. This was done mostly because I wanted to prolong my time getting to wear the suit of a politician, and partly because I was interested in what sort of books a Senator reads. Once I finally hunkered down and wrapped the leather couch up with sheets, I stayed up for a little while longer in that robe watching the news. It was a lot of pundit talk about Obama sealing the Democratic nod and what that meant for the Presidential election that would be taking place in almost four months.

When I finally did decide to turn in, I did so peacefully. Stretching my arms above my head to grasp the chain that would ultimately turn off the lamp, my eyes glanced over my shoulder and I felt safe under the watchful protection of those three figures just above my head. There, in front of me on the end table, was a photograph of Chris Dodd, Bill Clinton, and Al Gore playing golf. They would be watching me as I slept.

When morning finally came, I was greeted by the storm of a six year old plowing into the office ready to pounce on me in order to get me out of bed and up for breakfast. I quickly woke up and scampered off to the bathroom to get changed. Somewhere in life, I'm sure my mother taught me not to keep a Senator waiting. After folding the sheets and packing my bags, I went into the kitchen and discovered one last pleasant surprise. There behind the griddle was the Senator.

Senator Chris Dodd was making me pancakes.

# Boston

When we left the Dodd's, we had about one week left before reaching Boston, and those 140 miles would prove to be grueling. For those of you wishing to travel through the Nutmeg State, Connecticut is very beautiful, but the hills are rolling, which makes for very unpleasant walking. To add to our troubled spirits, we had no clue what we were going to do once we reached Boston. Back home we had some folks trying to pull through with some PR and news conferences, but it was summer vacation and three months into the trip. Unfortunately, most people back home had simply lost interest in keeping track of three people walking up the East Coast. But, then again, who can blame them? Walking isn't much of a spectator sport.

What was rather relieving during this last week were some of the folks we met in the Northeastern part of Connecticut. There was an older farm couple who had a pool they let us use for a few hours one afternoon, a woman named Jessica who took us home to play with her four children after meeting us at a garage sale on the side of the road, and finally Florence who gave us a bed at her home, which is located in the teacher housing section of a private boy's high school where her husband works.

Two days into the final week stretch, Kate received a phone call from our former host Jackie Dodd. Now that Jackie and Kate had become best friends forever, it seemed reasonable that she would be doing a little checking up on us every now and again. After they had chatted away about the beauties of their spawned friendship, Kate filled us in on some rather exciting news.

Apparently the same day that we had left the Dodd's, they had traveled North to a magical place known as Martha's Vineyard. Being the average guy that I am, I always thought that Martha's Vineyard was precisely that – a magical place that didn't really exist except for in the movies and fairytales. I thought it was just one of those pretentious terms people threw around to define any generic place where "cultured" people hung out on the weekends and took absurdly expensive holidays. But that day I learned that Martha's Vineyard is actually a real place. Who knew?

To our utter amazement, Senator Dodd had friends in high places that he frequented with in Martha's Vineyard. Okay, it wasn't amazing that Senator Dodd had high rolling friends, but it was amazing that they wanted to do something for us. One of those friends who wanted to do something for us just so happened to be the owner of the Liberty Hotel in Boston, Massachusetts. Having no experience with Boston and being unconnected with the "Hotel owner's crowd," I had no idea what to expect out of this place. All I really knew was that once we arrived at the Liberty Hotel, we would each get our own room, free of charge, for a two-night stay in Boston.

Walking across the street that separated Boston from the suburbs was indescribable. When I saw the skyscrapers of the city that peeked just above the horizon, I wanted to scream and cheer. I also wanted to hug every stranger around me and inform them of the magnitude of what had just happened. Unfortunately we were in the middle of a residential neighborhood and I didn't want to get the cops called on me for showing affection to my fellow human beings. So I did the next best thing and began calling every single person listed in my cell phone. When people couldn't be reached I snapped pictures and sent them in text messages with obnoxious words that looked like I was screaming, such as "YEAHHHHHH!!!" and "WOOOOOHHHHOOOOOO!!!" Sometimes I even used an excessive amount of exclamation points just to stress my enthusiasm, in case they couldn't fully grasp the experience.

Upon reaching what was conceivably the outer-edge of the downtown area, we called the Liberty Hotel. Because the hotel was a few blocks away from the capitol building, our final destination, they informed us that the house car would pick us up there in two hours, and that this should be about the same time it would take us to travel the rest of the distance. As we walked through Boston, we continually got curious looks much like we had been getting throughout the duration of the trip, which was understandable given that we were three walkers with giant backpacks and matching teal shirts walking through the middle of downtown Boston. However, this time was different because all that dirt, grime, and gear was now accompanied by a huge smile.

We reached the capitol at mid-day and were unexpectedly greeted by a local Sexual Assault Nurse Examiner and her husband who had come out to meet us after reading about our story in the newspaper that morning. It was nice having someone there to welcome us home.

After a brief photo shoot on the capitol steps with the three of us raising arms and giving each other over exaggerated high-fives, we sat on the steps and waited for the town car to arrive. While we were waiting, we noticed a local Fox affiliate about 50 yards from where we sat, and to our good fortune, there was also an anchor reporting outside. Feeling that we were newsworthy, Kate walked over and explained our situation. Ten minutes later, the anchor was making phone calls to her supervisors and interviewing us on the steps of the capitol for a story that would air later that night.

Just as the anchor was packing up her equipment, the town car for the Liberty Hotel, a black Cadillac with the limousine-tinted windows, was pulling onto the curb. An older gentleman got out an introduced himself as our driver. Taking our things and throwing them into the trunk one last time, we slipped into the well-groomed automobile, which visibly contrasted with our rather unkempt state.

The car ride was short, perhaps only five minutes, but in that time I managed to indulge myself in all the pleasantries our car afforded us. Excitedly, I read a copy of the *Boston Globe* that was tucked behind the driver's seat and listened to the driver's stories about all of the famous celebrities he had escorted to and from the Liberty Hotel.

The Liberty Hotel itself was sculpted out of the framework of an old prison. Pulling up to the front door, I could feel its awesome size consume me and the bars on the outside windows added to its novel appeal. When the car stopped, bagmen and bellboys surrounded the car in an instant and began opening every door and clearing out the trunk before I could even tuck the paper neatly back into the driver seat's pocket.

While exiting the car, one of them asked me for the name on the reservation. I told him kindly and reached for my bag. Unaware of the elite customs of the five-star hotel culture, I inadvertently began a tug-of-war over my belongings before the bagman finally informed me (in a tone that affirmed his annoyance with my behavior) that my bag would be waiting for me in my room. "Wow!" I thought, "Bags delivered to my room before I even had the keys!"

Entering the Liberty Hotel was an adventure all of its own. It was a palace of impeccable upkeep and glimmering everything. We took the escalator to the lobby floor and glanced around slowly and patiently making sure to enjoy every last detail of the scenery. I'm certain that the paying guests were as equally as intrigued with our appearance as we were with theirs. When we finally approached the front desk it was as if the receptionist had been waiting for our arrival, however, it was only noon and there was still another hour before check-in. So the receptionist called a PR representative to entertain us for a while.

When the representative, Katie, arrived at our side, she sat us down on a couch in the lobby and went over all the particulars.

"First, we should celebrate!" she exclaimed, "How about some champagne?"

Katie played her role as hotel historian and we all made small talk while opening an unreasonably priced bottle of champagne, drinking down a few extra-fancy bottles of water, and digging into hors d'oeuvres that I couldn't even pronounce.

"So, what do you all want to do now that you're here?" Katie asked.

Kate replied, "Well there were three things we had on our list to do once we hit Boston; get a massage, get a pedicure, and have a really nice dinner."

With this new information at hand, Katie excused herself and visited the concierge. Almost immediately, she returned with a wade of cash and a list of appointments.

"There's a pedicure place across the street. A masseuse will be in your room at one o'clock tomorrow after lunch. And I've made dinner reservation for you tonight for six o'clock in our five-star restaurant."

That was easy enough. We quickly got the keys for our rooms and headed across the street for a pedicure. On the way over I attempted to make conversation with Katie and innocently asked, "The women at the front desk gave us keys to the mini-bar. Are we going to get charged if we use it?"

To my delight Katie's reply was swift and to the point, "Just don't go crazy and you'll be all right." Ten dollar jelly beans, here I come!

After experiencing my first pedicure, I returned to the hotel while Kate and Rebecca were having their toes painted. Picking up a clean, authentic Liberty Hotel shirt from the front desk along with a razor and some shaving cream (my beard was way burly), I headed back to my room to relax before dinner. I turned on the news to watch for the coverage from our interview and proceeded to unpack all my dirty clothes and freshen up. Remarkably, the clothes were instantaneously picked up by housekeeping to be laundered.

Showered and shaved, I headed down to the lobby to meet up with Rebecca and Kate for dinner. Going through all the necessary steps of fine dinning – drinks, appetizers, meal, dessert – we unwound against the big city landscape overlooking downtown Boston, and I let the reality of it all sink in. This was it. We had arrived at our destination and we would no longer be waking up to the thought of having to walk 20 more miles. At the end of the meal, the waiter informed us that the hotel had taken care of the bill, and after leaving a gracious tip, we retired for the evening.

The following day was relaxing. I woke up early to the rising sun as it flooded into my 16th floor room through the ceiling to floor, wall-to-wall picture window. The town car was summoned and it took us back to where it had picked us up the day prior because we had an interviewed schedule for the Boston morning show on Fox around eight o'clock. It was perhaps only a five minute segment but, as I've mentioned before, any attention that can be generated for the issue of sexual violence and can get folks talking about how to be more proactive against sexual violence in their community is fine by me.

When I got back to the hotel, I picked up some plums at the front desk for breakfast. The receptionist had informed me that they usually did apples, but since plums were in season, it seemed intelligent to make the switch. I agreed. The plums were delicious and in a conservative estimate, I estimate that I ate about twelve over the course of our two days.

I spent most of the remainder of that day cooped up in my room, taking multiple showers, watching movies, reading, calling folks back home, and staring out the enormous, wall-to-wall window sixteen stories above the city. At around five o'clock I got hungry and ventured out to find myself some grub. I found a little hole-in-the-wall deli and got your basic turkey sandwich. I'm normally a vegetarian, but because of the extraordinary circumstances of the trip, I had to loosen up. For one, I simply find it disingenuous to refuse the hospitality of free food from hospitable strangers no matter what your eating habits. And two, we were on a budget and being a vegetarian can be expensive when trying to consume the amount of calories we burned each day. So I figured I had one more day to indulge my carnivorous-eating gene before returning to my regular routine of fruits and vegetables.

After getting my sandwich, I took the long way back from the deli and enjoyed the cobblestone streets before stumbling across a Walgreens where I figured I would grab a beverage to go with dinner. Next to the entrance of this store was a man asking for change and I told him I'd get him on the way out. Upon exiting, I handed him a bag with a couple Gatorades in it and a big bag of pretzels. Dumping the change from a broken dollar into his coffee cup, I asked him if I could sit for a minute and enjoy my dinner with him on the sidewalk. He agreed.

In all, I probably sat with Dennis for almost three hours that night. It's amazing the stories you'll hear when you're willing to just sit and listen. When someone senses your genuine desire to enter into their experiences with them, they are free to cut out all the conversational foreplay of small talk and get right to the point.

Without disclosing too much about Dennis' personal situation and struggles, it's safe to say that he had simply fallen on rough times. Interested, I asked about how the city of Boston treated folks who were homeless.

"Not well," was his brief reply.

He informed me that the shelters were few and far between and that he had recently been kicked out of one due to his own short-comings with drugs and alcohol. I admired his honesty. In fact, I admire the honesty of most folks who are homeless. In my limited experience, I would guess that their honesty is rooted in complete vulnerability. When society already thinks so little of you, what do you have to lose by being completely honest with everyone about everything? Sure some folks might lie about what they're going to use that extra change for, but as far as why they are in particular situations, they seem to be rather honest. We could all learn an important lesson from this.

Anyway, as I was saying, Dennis and I just sat there like two old friends enjoying the cooling night as the sun slipped behind the skyscrapers. It was almost as if we had once known each other long ago and were now stuck in that moment where you feel the need to fill in an old friend about the last ten years of your life. Sitting next to him in my brand new Liberty Hotel shirt, I told him similar versions of the stories you have just read. I even told him about Senator Dodd and our good fortune with the Liberty Hotel.

After going back and forth like this for a while, Dennis finally asked if he could borrow my cell phone in order to call up a few friends and his father. I briefly spoke to all of them and they all spoke to me as if cued by a social worker and kept warning me of the dangers and pitfalls of hanging out on the streets at night. I politely took their advice while pushing it into the back of my mind. I know they had my best interest in mind, but I did just walk the length of the East Coast and if I had learned anything, it was that hanging out on the streets and talking to strangers may get you a hot meal and bed to sleep in.

With night rushing upon us it suddenly dawned on me that Dennis was without a blanket and had very few clean clothes. Telling him to stay put, I rushed back to my hotel room to collect what few items I had. Call me crazy, but it was my feeling that our supplies had been given to us with the expressed purpose of walking the East Coast. Now that the trip was over, I felt that Dennis' needs were some sort of sign to pass those belongings along. I gathered up what I could, and after stopping at the front desk for some extra plums, I headed back to the Walgreens.

Getting back to my place on the sidewalk, I presented Dennis with four pairs of socks, a t-shirt, a poncho, a sleeping bag, and a few plums. He thanked me graciously, and after we had enjoyed a plum together, he gathered up his belongings, slipped around the corner, and off into the night.

I don't know what happened to Dennis after that. I had given him my address in the hopes that he would write, but so far nothing has come through the mail. But then again, I suppose that's how relationships work sometimes. In any case, that was how this walk had worked most of the time. For a moment, you enter into somebody's life, try to connect in a way where both people will feel loved, accepted, and validated for who they are in that moment, and when the moment has passed, one of you will inevitably slip around a corner and off into the night.

# Epilogue

The morning after Dennis and I had hung out, I met Kate and Rebecca down stairs along with a few representatives from the Liberty Hotel. We took quite an abundant amount of pictures with several different people in several different locations. I'm sure they used some of those shots for public relations work, which is completely okay by me because they sure did earn it after putting us up for two days.

The bellboy whistled for a cab in the morning drizzle, and we were getting ready for the final chapter of our trip – the ride home. Having changed our dates around a couple of different times, we were now opting out of the plane ride home and heading to the nearest rent-a-car, which was coincidentally enough also located at the airport. In all, the drive would take almost fourteen hours, but it was worth not having to wait around Boston for another few days. We were tired, worn out, and really wanted to get home.

The ride back included a few detours, which consisted of a tattoo shop and a late-night screening of the newest Batman movie, but we finally made it back home and parted with final goodbyes and final good lucks. During this time it was unspoken, yet mutually agreed upon, that we would avoid contact with each other for the next few weeks. Sometimes that space is just needed after being around someone day and night for three months.

Being home was utterly surreal, but I quickly returned to my usual routine and began getting ready to move back up to school. Contrary to my sense of entitlement and enlightenment, my professors were not going to delay the start of classes just because I wanted some time off to reflect on my life-changing experience. Because of that, this book is the first real opportunity I've had to sit down with myself and reflect on what ended almost a year ago. Sure, I've shared stories with friends and presented the material at conferences, but speaking for an audience and speaking to yourself are two completely different things. Now that I've had this time to myself, this is what I have learned.

The walk wasn't about us. It was never about us. The walk was about survivors. At the end of the day, the only thing that remains important about our act of walking, or any act of resistance, was whether or not it had the ability to call attention to sexual violence and create dialogue about a social system rooted in patriarchal domination that remains in desperate need of much repair.

For me, walking the East Coast wasn't even about changing laws or creating political platforms surrounding the issue of sexual violence. The laws and politics are and have been in place for a while now: it is illegal to engage in any act of sexual violence toward anyone. However, the laws are only as effective as they are enforced in society and into social acceptance. Social consciousness must be weaved into the social fabric of our culture in order for the greater population to demand that the laws be upheld. Therefore, walking the East Coast was not about changing the laws insomuch as it was about changing people's attitudes – changing people's hearts. With each step I took, I wasn't thinking about how to stop bad people from committing bad acts, I was thinking about how to engage good people in acts of resistance.

My struggle was and remains a struggle against indifference. In reality, pulling good people out of their trance of social apathy is much more difficult and requires a great deal more of creativity than convincing an abuser that what he or she is doing is wrong. Most abusers know that what they do is wrong. On the other hand, good people don't always understand that sexual violence is an issue that affects friends, roommates, sons, daughters, teachers, doctors, parents, sisters, cashiers, housekeepers, government employees, and everyone else not mentioned on this list, every single day!

I do not consider myself a great or wise person, but I do consider myself honest and my efforts sincere. As I see it, sexual violence is an issue in our culture that most people unapologetically dismiss, and to continue to collectively turn a blind eye is shameful. Everyday ordinary folks silently overlook sexist behavior, laugh at rape jokes, purchase objectifying media, call women bitches, and, simply stated, don't outwardly give a damn. We should all be ashamed. But there is hope.

It should also be noted that the walk wasn't special in any way where we or it should be elevated as heroic or better than the efforts of anyone else working against sexual violence. The walk was simply our creative way to grab people's attention. After all the physical, emotional, mental, and spiritual pain that went into the walk, what I learned is that if you want to entice change, you don't have to walk the East Coast! This was a hard, sole splitting lesson to swallow.

However, you must do something! Even if your action is as simple as correcting dehumanizing language or getting a bunch of friends together and committing to wear teal colored shirts one day every week, we all must do our part in sparking dialogue and enticing change. Sexual violence is pervasive in our communities, and unless we do something to disrupt this accepted cultural pattern that encourages violence, the culture will continue forward unchallenged.

With that, those of us who understand the cultural pervasiveness of sexual violence cannot allow ourselves to become silent because silence only communicates our acceptance with the status quo. I recognize that finding your voice in a culture that ask you to sit down, to shut up, and to conform to the oppressive structures that continuously assault our fellow human beings is no easy task. And speaking up against sexual violence, derogatory images, and dehumanizing language that are laced throughout our culture, will most likely cause you a great deal of sacrifice and a great deal of criticism. But all I ask is that you reflect on your priorities. Is it more important to fit in, or is it more important to gain the respect of survivors? We must face our social discomfort with confrontation and ask ourselves, "At what cost do I remain silent?"

"At *whose* cost do I remain silent?"

We must be *actively against* instead of *passively for* sexual violence. We all need to find our own ways to get creative in our communities, and discover ways that continually draw healthy, loving, and positive attention to the issue. Once you've sparked conversation between you and your neighbor as to why you're acting differently, why you're dressed differently, or why you're – in our case – walking the East Coast, that's when you let the message take over.

Years from now those individuals I met during the summer of 2008 may not remember us, but they will remember that one summer day when three walkers passed through their town trying to ignite passion against sexual violence. They will remember the message. They will remember that somebody cared and that somebody tried to end sexual violence – one step at a time.

Joshua Daniel Phillips
May 2009

# Influential Readings

Gandhi once said, "I have nothing new to teach the world. Truth and Non-violence are as old as the hills. All I have done is to try experiments in both on as vast a scale as I could." With these words of humility always fresh at the front of my mind, I am constantly reminded of how presumptuous it would be of me to ever claim that the words I have shared or that the lessons I have learned were ever anything more than complied wisdom of those who have come before me. Therefore, I think it is wise and respectable to include the following list. These books represent only a *very* short list of some of the authors and the writings that continue to inspire me. Because it would be overwhelming to list all the books that I find fantastic and extraordinary, I have done my best to give you a small taste of my recommendations in hopes that you may pursue more literature, essays, and knowledge about the following authors and their researched topics.

In no particular order:

*No Greater Love*, Mother Teresa

*Gandhi: His Life and Message for the World*, Louis Fischer

*The Autobiography of Malcolm X as told by Alex Haley*

*Out of Solitude: Three Meditations on the Christian Life*, Henri Nouwen

*The Book of Luke*, as discussed with the folks at Alternative Seminary, Philadelphia, PA

*Another Country*, James Baldwin

*Life is a Miracle: An Essay Against Modern Superstition*, Wendell Berry

*All About Love: New Visions*, bell hooks

*Life Together*, Dietrich Bonhoeffer

*Bury My Heart at Wounded Knee*, Dee Brown

*Freedom of Simplicity: Finding Harmony in a Complex World*, Richard Foster

*Sister Outsider: Essays and Speeches*, Audre Lorde

*John Brown*, W.E.B. DuBois

*The Bhagavad Gita*

*Peace Pilgrim: Her Life and Work in Her Own Words*, Peace Pilgrim

*The Irresistible Revolution*, Shane Claiborne

*Of Mice and Men*, John Steinbeck, as read to me by my dad when I was 10 years old

# About the Author

**Joshua Phillips** has been actively advocating against sexual violence since 2003 when he joined an advocacy group at Central Michigan University. Since then, he has had the privilege of presenting numerous programs on campuses and in communities throughout the United States. Between his undergraduate and graduate work, Josh took a year to volunteer in Camden, New Jersey with the organization Mission Year where he worked at a homeless shelter and ran after-school programs. After returning to Central Michigan in 2007, Josh earned a Master of Arts in Communication. He is currently living in Southern Illinois as a volunteer, an advocate, a community member, and an educator, as he continues to experiment with attention calling actions in an effort to create dialogue and spark change in and around his community. Joshua's hope is to use stories from the walk to inspire others to creatively engage in everyday activism by creating dialogue about social justice and the issues that affect us all.

Joshua may be contacted at: joshua.d.phillips@hotmail.com

# BUY A SHARE OF THE FUTURE IN YOUR COMMUNITY

These certificates make great holiday, graduation and birthday gifts that can be personalized with the recipient's name. The cost of one S.H.A.R.E. or one square foot is $54.17. The personalized certificate is suitable for framing and will state the number of shares purchased and the amount of each share, as well as the recipient's name. The home that you participate in "building" will last for many years and will continue to grow in value.

**Here is a sample SHARE certificate:**

## YES, I WOULD LIKE TO HELP!

*I support the work that Habitat for Humanity does and I want to be part of the excitement! As a donor, I will receive periodic updates on your construction activities but, more importantly, I know my gift will help a family in our community realize the dream of homeownership.* **I would like to SHARE in your efforts against substandard housing in my community!** *(Please print below)*

PLEASE SEND ME _____ SHARES at $54.17 EACH = $ $_____

*In Honor Of:* _____

*Occasion: (Circle One)*    *HOLIDAY*    *BIRTHDAY*    *ANNIVERSARY*

     *OTHER:* _____

*Address of Recipient:* _____

*Gift From:* _____ *Donor Address:* _____

*Donor Email:* _____

**I AM ENCLOSING A CHECK FOR $ $_____ PAYABLE TO HABITAT FOR HUMANITY OR PLEASE CHARGE MY VISA OR MASTERCARD** *(CIRCLE ONE)*

Card Number _____ Expiration Date: _____

Name as it appears on Credit Card _____ Charge Amount $ _____

Signature _____

Billing Address _____

Telephone # Day _____ Eve _____

**PLEASE NOTE:** Your contribution is tax-deductible to the fullest extent allowed by law.
**Habitat for Humanity • P.O. Box 1443 • Newport News, VA 23601 • 757-596-5553**
**www.HelpHabitatforHumanity.org**

9 781600 376771